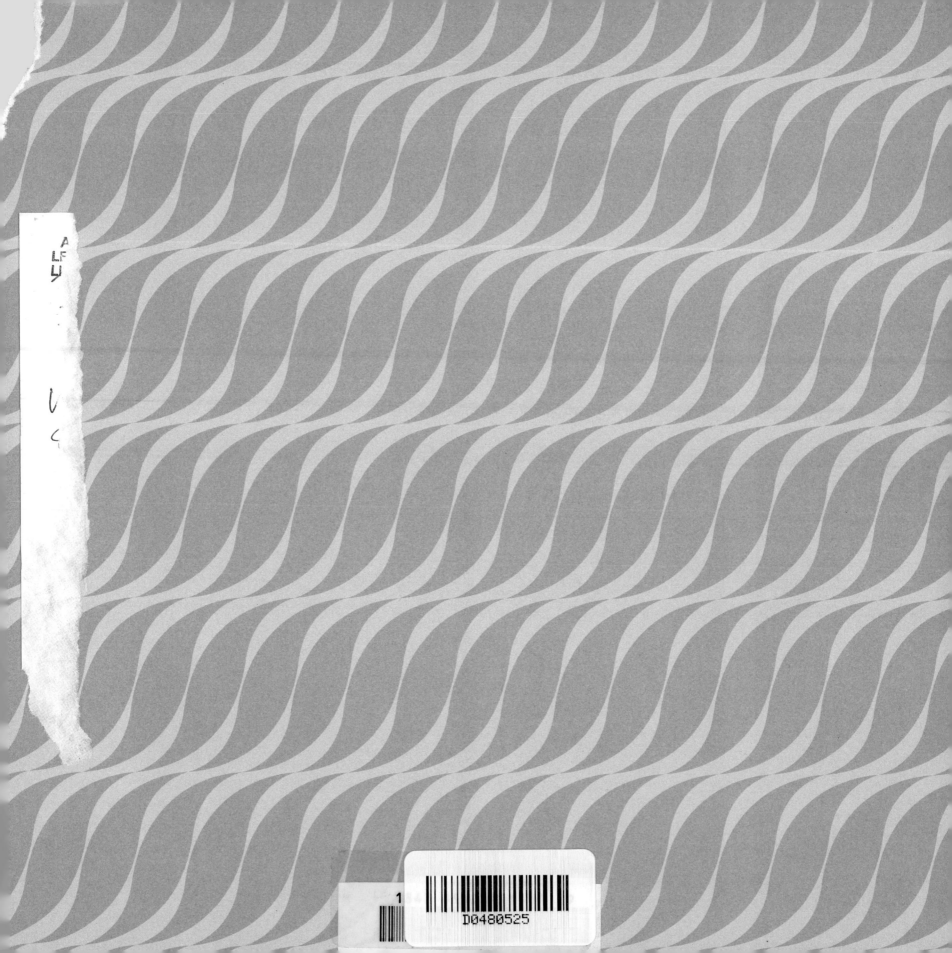

ANNUALS & PERENNIALS

ANNUALS & PERENNIALS

The gardener's complete guide to bedding plants

Richard Bird

southwater

This edition is published by Southwater

Distributed in the UK by
The Manning Partnership
251-253 London Road East, Batheaston,
Bath BA1 7RL, UK
tel. (0044) 01225 852 727
fax. (0044) 01225 852 852

Distributed in the USA by
Ottenheimer Publishing
5 Park Center Court, Suite 300
Owing Mills, MD 2117-5001, USA
tel. (001) 410 902 9100
fax. (001) 410 902 7210

Distributed in Australia by
Sandstone Publishing
Unit 1, 360 Norton Street, Leichhardt
New South Wales 2040 Australia
tel.(0061) 2 9560 7888
fax. (0061) 2 9560 7488

Distributed in New Zealand by
Five Mile Press NZ,
PO Box 33-1071, Takapuna
Auckland 9, New Zealand
tel. (0064) 9 4444 144
fax. (0064) 9 4444 518

Southwater is an imprint of Anness Publishing Limted
©2000 Anness Publishing Limited

Printed and bound in Hong Kong

1 3 5 7 9 10 8 6 4 2

Publisher: Joanna Lorenz
Project Editor: Emma Hardy
Copy Editor: Alison Bolus
Designer: Julie Francis
Production Controller: Joanna King
Photographer: Jonathan Buckley

Previously published in two separate volumes, *Annuals* and *Perennials*

Publisher's note: In the United States, throughout the Sun Belt states, from Florida,
across the Gulf Coast, south Texas, southern deserts to Southern California and
coastal regions, annuals are planted in the autumn, bloom in the winter and
spring, and die at the beginning of summer.

Half title page: Love-in-a-mist, a beautifully intricate annual, is typically a delicate light blue.
Frontispiece: A late summer border, filled with perennials.
Title page: This orange *Osteospermum* gives a bright splash of colour.
Above: A daylily (*Hemerocallis*) peeps through the delicate silver foliage of an *Artemisia*.
Opposite: An informal mixture of annuals and perennials draws the eye along a path to the front door.

CONTENTS

pelargoniums, are treated as annuals as they are unable to withstand a cold winter and are usually started again each year. Similarly short-lived perennials such as sweet williams and wallflowers are treated as annuals and grown from seed every year. All these provide a rich source of material for a varied and very colourful garden.

Perennials, on the other hand are plants that go on growing from one year to the next. Woody plants, such as trees and shrubs are usually excluded from this category, as are alpines and bulbs. Sometimes the terms "herbaceous plants or perennials" are used, meaning that the plants die back and reappear each year.

Above: *White shasta daises* (Leucanthemum × superbum*) create a delicate contrast with the tall spires of hollyhocks* (Alcea*) and mullein* (Verbascum chaixii)*, all in pale yellow and white shades.*

The term "perennial" is usually restricted to those plants that die back below ground either completely or partially each year. Very few people grow exclusively perennials and it is usually accepted that certain plants from other categories are included within the general term. Thus shrubs like fuchsias and Cestrum parqui, which are often cut to the ground by frosts, are included. Larger bulbs, such as lilies, are also included. That the boundaries of definition are somewhat blurred does not matter at all; as gardeners we are out to enjoy our plants and the effects that we can create with them, rather than worry too much about botanical niceties.

By their very nature perennials are longer-lived plants than annuals and therefore form part of a more permanent

Above: *Contrasting purple and white perennials create a very striking mixed border.*

Left: *A stone urn filled with pelargoniums and lobelia, surrounded by ivy and ferns.*

garden. One thinks in the longer term when planning with perennials as opposed to from year to year with annuals. Since it is going to be basically the same from year to year it is important to get it right as you will have to live with it. You can, of course, alter things around, but they may take a while to settle down again, so planning is essential if you want to get it right first time. It is a bit like decorating a room. For many reasons you do not want to redecorate or change the furnishing (the perennials) every year, but you can easily choose a different form of Christmas decorations (the annuals) each year.

Both annuals and perennials can be mixed in with each other as well as other plants, there is no rule that says you must grow one or the other. Annuals are particularly useful for providing instant, and often bright colour as well as having a long season. Perennials can display not only a wonderful range of colours, many of them subtle, but also provide superb foliage effects. The flowering season for individual perennial plants is shorter, but the plant often has more to offer than just the flowers: shape and texture of the foliage being two other key factors. These will often still be effective long after flowering is over. Annuals can be mixed with the perennials to fill temporary gaps or to provide continuing colour throughout the season. The coming and

Above: *This beautiful* Schizostylus coccinea *is an autumn bulb which is usually regarded as a perennial.*

Above: *Pelargoniums are available in a wide range of striking reds, varying from orange red through to scarlet and crimson.*

going of perennial flowers means that the border can be an ever changing scene, the addition of annuals adds longer periods of colour. Shrubs and trees can also be included. These form a permanent structure to the garden or individual border around which the perennials and annuals provide a changing scene of interest.

Above: *Where two colours strongly contrast, as in this* nemesia strimosa, *the overall effect is startling and eyecatching.*

Right: *A cottage garden with mixed with annuals and perennials.*

There are different techniques in dealing with annuals and perennials, but neither type are difficult to grow. In spite of the wide range of tools and gadgets at garden centres, surprising little equipment is needed to produce a flower garden. If you grow your own plants, which, again, is not at all difficult, you can buy propagators and greenhouses, but much can be achieved with polythene bags and kitchen window sills. There will be failures with plants, both in the propagation and the growing of them in the borders, but even the experts have problems. Gardening is one of the things that you learn about without realising you are learning. Just by going out into the garden and getting on with it you will be able to produce a very acceptable bed or hanging basket of annuals and perennials. Gradually as you learn you will produce better and better results. If you have failures, shrug your shoulders and start again; in gardening there is always another year.

Increasing garden centres and nurseries are selling plants by their Latin names rather than their English ones. Many gardeners, especially new ones, worry about this, but like the techniques involved, they are things that one gradually learns. After all there can be very few people, let alone gardeners, who do not know the names Rhododendron, Chrysanthemum, Fuchsia or Delphinium. These are not exactly ordinary English words and yet we are all so familiar with them that we accept them and do not think twice about using them. Once you start growing perennials and annuals many other names will also become familiar. In this book we use both English and Latin names, but inevitably there are some plants that do not have an English name and we have had to rely on the Latin only.

This book shows some of the wide range of possibilities and helps to stimulate the imagination to help you design a colourful garden. It also helps on the practical side so that you are able to achieve what you already see in your minds eye.

GARDENING TECHNIQUES

The techniques needed to grow annuals and perennials
are relatively simple and often require no more than a
little common sense. In this section of the book, as
well as explaining how to grow annuals and
perennials, there are detailed instructions on
preparing the soil ready for planting, weeding,
mulching and watering and feeding. There is also
guidance on specific techniques for annuals
and perennials including pinching out and
dead-heading and staking and protecting.
Learning comes with practice, so use this section
as a helpful starting point, but to really know and
understand your plants and garden, you will have
to go outside and get your hands dirty!

Left: *Many varieties of primulas brighten up the garden in
late winter and early spring.*

Preparing the Ground

There can be no doubt that the soil is the most important ingredient when it comes to creating a garden. Understanding your soil and treating it with care and attention will reap rewards that are impossible to achieve in any other way.

CLEARING THE GROUND

The first task when starting any garden is to clear the ground. The most likely problem will be weeds, but in many new gardens there will be builder's rubbish, such as bricks, and, worse still, discarded plaster, which can cause problems by making the soil very alkaline. This may not be a problem if you already live on a chalky (alkaline) soil, but it can be a nuisance if you have a neutral or acid soil and want to grow ericaceous and other acid-loving plants.

If you have recently acquired an older garden, you may well find that all manner of rubbish has been dumped in it over the years by previous owners who were not gardeners. Do not make a half-hearted attempt to get rid of this. Hire a skip, if necessary, and have it all taken away. It may seem a lot of trouble, but once it is done you will be rid of the problem. If you leave rubbish lying around at this stage it will be more difficult to deal with once the garden is planted.

DEALING WITH WEEDS

The next problem is the weeds. Perennials are often in the soil in the same place for several, if not many, years, and if weeds, perennial ones in particular, find their way into the roots of these plants the only sure way of getting rid of them is to dig up the plant as well. If you don't do this, but simply break the weeds off where they enter the plant, they will soon revive and you will have a constant battle on your hands. More people give up gardening or are bored by it because of weeds than for any other reason.

You must get rid of all the weeds properly. There is no point in just scraping them off the surface because they will quickly regenerate from the remaining roots. They have to be either totally removed or killed. If the soil in your garden is light and crumbly, it is possible to remove the weeds as you dig. On heavier soils you can either cover the ground with an impermeable mulch such as thick black polythene for several months, or use a weedkiller. Most gardeners are now rightly unwilling to use too many chemicals in the garden, but, if it is done properly, it will only need to be done once. Always follow the manufacturer's instructions to the letter.

Dig the soil, adding as much well-rotted organic material as possible. If you can, carry out this digging in the autumn and leave the ground until spring before planting. If you do this you will see, and be able to remove, any weeds that have regrown from roots that were missed before.

1 Since perennial beds will be basically undisturbed for many years, it is important to clear the area of any weeds by spraying with weedkiller.

2 You can also clear the area of weeds by organic means, either by skimming off the surface or covering it with black polythene for several months.

3 Dig the first trench to one spade's depth across the plot, and barrow the soil you have removed to the other end of the plot where it will be used to fill in the final trench.

4 Fork a layer of well-rotted compost or manure into the bottom of the trench to improve the soil structure and to provide nutrients for the plants.

5 Dig the next trench across the plot, turning the soil on to the compost in the first trench. Add compost to the new trench and then dig the next.

6 Continue down the border until the whole of the surface has been turned. Add some compost to the final trench and then fill it in with the soil taken from the first.

7 If possible, dig in the autumn and allow the winter weather to break down the soil. In spring, take out any resprouted weeds and rake over the bed.

Conditioning the Soil

To maintain a healthy soil, you must replace the nutrients used by your growing plants. Nature replenishes the soil all the time, and it is important to emulate this in the garden. In the wild, plants are constantly dying back or dropping their leaves, and as they do so, the previous year's lush green growth decays and rots down, returning the nutrients to the soil. In the normal course of things, little is removed from the cycle and plants have a constant supply of the nutrients that are vital to their health and growth.

RECYCLING GARDEN WASTE

The careless gardener discards all the old foliage and stems into the dustbin (garbage can) or burns them, and so the garden waste is not returned to the soil to become available for future generations of plants. Unless action is taken to redress this, the soil becomes impoverished and plants become thin and sickly, and are difficult to grow.

The prudent gardener, on the other hand, recycles as much as possible by composting all garden waste and then spreading or digging it into the ground to return it to the soil. Because gardeners remove some of the plant material in the way of cut flowers or vegetables, they should introduce extra material, such as farmyard manure, to supplement the garden compost. In this way, the plants are provided with the nutrients that they need.

SOIL STRUCTURE

Another important aspect to consider is the structure of the soil. Heavy, compacted soils are not particularly good for growing plants. On the other hand, light,

sandy ones also have their problems in that they tend to dry out quickly and the nutrients are leached (washed) out during wet weather. With both extremes of soil type, it is important that the structure of the soil is modified to provide the best possible conditions. Fortunately, this is possible, although in the more extreme circumstances it will take a number of years before the benefits are really seen.

SOIL NUTRITION

To some extent, feeding and conditioning the soil can be achieved in the same way. The addition of rotted organic material such as garden compost not only provides nutrients but also helps to retain moisture in light soils and breaks down the structure of heavier soils.

It is important that the material is well rotted before it is added to the garden, because waste material actually requires nitrogen during the breaking-down process, and, if it is not sufficiently broken down, it will extract nitrogen from the soil so that it can complete the process; this is the reverse of what the gardener wants.

Above: *By providing the best possible soil conditions that you can, you are making certain that the border will be fertile and produce the best possible results.*

ADDING HUMUS

1 As much well-rotted compost or farmyard manure as possible should be added to the bed, especially at the time that it is dug.

2 You can leave it as a mulch for the worms to work into the soil, or you can lightly fork it into the surface.

3 For an existing bed, top-dress the soil with a good layer of well-rotted compost or farmyard manure. Leaf mould and seaweed also make excellent additions.

SOIL CONDITIONERS

Chipped or composted bark has little nutritional value but it is an excellent mulch.

Farmyard manure is rich in nutrients but it also often contains weed seed. Manure also makes a good soil conditioner.

Garden compost, which can be made from all garden waste and the uncooked vegetable peelings from the kitchen, has good nutrient value and is a good soil conditioner.

Leafmould made from composted leaves has good nutritional value and is a good conditioner and mulch.

Peat is not suitable because it breaks down too quickly and has little nutritional value.

Proprietary (commercial) soil conditioners are of variable quality but are usually nutritious conditioners.

Seaweed is rich in minerals and is a good conditioner.

Spent hops, which are the waste from breweries, have some nutritional value and are a good mulch and conditioner.

Spent mushroom compost is good for mulching but usually contains chalk or lime.

COMPOST

The best material to use when making compost is undoubtedly what came from the soil in the first place – that is, all dead plant material, grass clippings, shredded hedge clippings and prunings. This can be piled into a heap and left to rot down, although most gardeners prefer to use a compost bin. These are wooden or plastic structures into which all the garden waste is placed. The bins should have holes in the side to allow in air.

Any garden waste can be used, as long as it is not too woody and is not diseased. Do not add the roots of perennial weeds, and make sure that all waste is free of seeds. In theory, the compost should get hot enough as it breaks down to kill these off, but, in practice, it rarely does and they are liable to germinate wherever the compost is spread. Vegetable peelings and other non-cooked vegetable waste from the kitchen can also be used.

Do not use the compost too early; remember that it should be well rotted before being added to the garden. A good indication that it is ready is that it no longer smells or has a slightly sweet smell. The compost should be dug into the soil in the autumn when you are preparing the beds and borders. In established beds, it can be worked into the soil around the plants or left on the surface for the worms to carry down.

A good substitute for garden compost is well-rotted farmyard manure, if you can obtain ready supplies. This is animal waste, usually mixed with straw or wood shavings, although it sometimes includes hay, which can be a nuisance if it was allowed to seed before cutting.

Leafmould is another useful material. Collect and rot down your own leaves; never take leafmould from local woods, because you will break the natural cycle and impoverish the soil. Spent mushroom compost is another good material, especially for top-dressing borders, but it usually has lime added to it, so do not apply it where you grow acid-loving plants.

FERTILIZERS

Fertilizers can also be used to add nutrients to the soil, but they do not help to improve the structure of the soil in the same way that fibrous material does. There are two classes of fertilizer – organic and inorganic. Organic fertilizers, which are derived from live materials, such as old bones or blood, usually release their nutrients slowly. Inorganic fertilizers are derived from minerals in rock. They are made purely from chemicals, and, although they are quick acting, tend to get washed from the soil quickly.

ACID AND ALKALINE SOILS

Very few gardeners attempt to change the alkalinity or acidity of the flower borders, although this is much more important in the vegetable garden. In extremely acid gardens, however, it may be desirable to add some lime. Check the conditions with a soil testing kit and then follow the dosage recommended by the manufacturer on the packet.

If you have alkaline soil, and you want to grow acid-loving plants, rather than trying to change the pH value of your soil, your best option is to grow them in containers.

ADDING FERTILIZER

The best fertilizer is organic material because it improves the structure, as well as the fertility, of the soil. However, if this is not available, use an organic, slow-release fertilizer, such as bonemeal, to feed the soil.

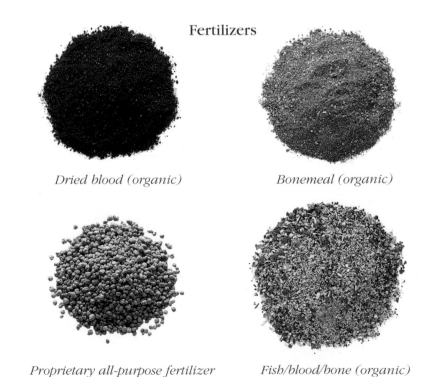

Fertilizers

Dried blood (organic)

Bonemeal (organic)

Proprietary all-purpose fertilizer (inorganic)

Fish/blood/bone (organic)

MAKING COMPOST

1 Compost any soft-stemmed garden waste except seed and perennial weeds. Tougher materials, such as hedge trimmings, should be shredded first. You can also add uncooked vegetable waste.

2 Regularly turn the contents of the compost bin and, when full, cover with polythene (plastic) until the contents have broken down. Alternatively, cover it with soil and plant marrows or courgettes on the top of the bin.

3 The contents should break down, leaving a crumbly, non-sticky, non-smelling compost that is ideal for adding to the soil or using as a mulch.

IMPROVING DRAINAGE

To help heavy soils break down more readily and allow the free drainage of excess water, add sharp sand or fine gravel and fork it into the surface layer.

ALTERING ACIDITY

Although it is not as important as in the vegetable garden, you may need to lower the acidity of the soil. This can be done by adding lime at the recommended dosage.

Sowing Seed

Growing plants from seed is one of the easiest and cheapest ways of getting a lot of new plants. The techniques involved are not at all difficult, even for those who believe that they do not have green fingers.

THE BEST APPROACH

A packet of seed is relatively cheap when you consider the number of plants you will get from it. There is one disadvantage, however. Plants grown from seed do not always resemble the parent from which the seed was collected. If, for example, you collect the seed of a white hardy geranium, with the intention of growing more, you may find that the whole batch of seedlings produces purple flowers. On the other hand, plants grown by vegetative means – that is, by

taking cuttings or by division – always resemble the parent plant. Thus, dividing a white geranium will provide white offspring.

Therefore, if you want to produce a bed of, say, a dozen plants, all of a consistent colour, it is best to use vegetative propagation, unless the plant is known to come true from seed. Remember, too, that it is not only the colour of the flowers that may vary: the colour and shape of the leaves, as well as the size and shape of the whole plant, may also be different.

It is not always a bad thing to grow something unexpected, of course. You may, for instance, suddenly get a blue-flowered form from your white-flowered plant, which may be a plant that is not already in cultivation. It is always rewarding to grow something that no one else will have in their garden. In fact, many of the cultivars we see today were originally chance seedlings that simply appeared in somebody's garden. You may be interested in experimenting in this way, or you may simply feel that a slight variation in the colour and size of the plants does not really matter.

OBTAINING SEED

There are various sources of seed. Many gardeners rely on the major seed merchants, who produce coloured catalogues listing all their available seed. You will get a much wider choice of plants if you order from the catalogues than if you go to your local garden centre, which can carry only a fraction of the bigger merchants' stock.

Another way of obtaining seed is to join a society that runs seed exchange schemes. These often list thousands of species and include many rarer plants. If you want even rarer and more unusual plants, seeds can be obtained by taking shares in the seed-hunting expeditions in the wild that are often advertised in gardening magazines. These work out to be remarkably

Left: *Sisyrinchiums are among the many perennials that can be sown in open ground.*

inexpensive per packet of seed, but you often have to take pot luck about what is gathered.

Having acquired your seeds, there are two ways of dealing with them. They can be sown in the open ground or in pots. For small quantities and the more difficult plants, pots are preferable, but for bulk growing of the more common garden plants, sowing directly into the soil is far less bother and much less expensive because you will not need to buy pots and potting compost (soil mix).

Perennials and biennials can be sown where they are to flower, but it is more usual to sow them in a nursery bed and transplant them to their final positions when they are large enough to move.

SOWING IN THE OPEN

Prepare the bed thoroughly by digging the soil and removing all the weeds, then break it down into a fine tilth with a rake. Sow the seed in spring, as the soil begins to warm up. Draw out a shallow drill about 1cm (½in) deep with the corner of a hoe, using a garden line to keep it straight. If the soil is dry, water, and let the water soak away before sowing. Sow thinly along the row, mark the ends with labels and then rake the soil back into the drill. Remember to water the bed in dry weather and to keep it weeded. When the seedlings have grown to a manageable size, thin them to distances of at least 15cm (6in).

Most species will be ready to plant out in their flowering position during the following autumn.

SOWING SEED IN OPEN GROUND

1 Prepare the soil carefully, thoroughly removing all weeds and breaking it down into a fine tilth with a rake.

2 Draw out a shallow drill with a corner of a hoe. It should be about 1cm (½in) deep. Keep the drill straight by using a garden line as a guide.

3 If the soil is dry, water the drill with a watering can and wait until the water has soaked in before sowing.

4 It is essential to mark the ends of the row, so that you know where it is when it comes to hoeing as well as to identify the plants you have sown.

5 Sow the seed thinly along the drill. Larger seed can be station sown at intervals, which means that there there will be no need to thin.

6 Gently rake the soil back into the drill, covering over the seed. In dry weather, do not allow the soil to dry out.

SEED FOR SOWING IN OPEN GROUND

Agastache (giant hyssop)
Alcea (hollyhock)
Anthemis tinctoria
  (golden marguerite)
Aquilegia (columbine)
Astrantia (masterwort)
Bupleurum falcatum
  (sickle-leaved hare's ear)
Centranthus ruber
  (red valerian)
Corydalis lutea;
  C. ochroleuca
Delphinium
Digitalis (foxglove; this
  plant is poisonous)
Foeniculum (fennel)
Helleborus (hellebore)
Lupinus (lupin)
Lychnis (catchfly)
Myosotis (forget-me-not)
Physostegia (obedient
  plant)
Polemonium (Jacob's
  ladder)
Primula
Pulsatilla (pasqueflower)
Silene (campion, catchfly)
Sisyrinchium striatum
Thalictrum aquilegiifolium
Verbascum (mullein)
Verbena
Viola

Sowing in Pots

If you do not have space in the garden to devote to seed beds, you may choose to grow seeds in pots. Small pots will usually produce enough seedlings for most gardening needs, and even large bedding schemes can easily be filled with annuals from a few trays.

THE ADVANTAGES

It is usually sufficient to sow perennials in a 9cm (3½in) pot, which will produce thirty or more seedlings. For annuals, a tray or half-tray will produce hundreds of seedlings.

Whichever method you choose, fill the pot or tray to the rim with compost (soil mix) and then tap it on the bench to settle it. Lightly press down the compost (soil mix) so that it is level. Sow the seed thinly on the compost (soil mix) and then cover it with a layer of fine gravel or grit. Label the pot and water it from above with a watering can or from below by standing the pot in a shallow tray of water.

Place the pot in a sheltered spot, away from direct sun.

Annuals should be covered with a piece of glass or cling film (plastic wrap) or enclosed in a plastic bag.

There is no need to use a propagator as perennials and annuals will germinate at normal temperatures, although this would speed up the process. Germination will take from a few days to two or three years for some perennials. The seed of some perennials requires a winter's cold weather before germination will occur. Keep the pots watered. Most seeds can be sown in early spring. Some perennials, however, such as primulas and hellebores, need to be sown fresh – that is, as soon as the seed ripens – which usually means sowing in late summer or autumn.

1 The equipment you will need to sow the seed includes a selection of pots or trays, a good-quality sowing compost (soil mix), a propagator (optional), and your choice of seed.

2 Fill a pot or tray with compost (soil mix). Tap down to settle it and lightly flatten the surface with the base of a pot.

3 Sow the seed thinly on the surface. If you need a lot of plants, do not sow thickly, but use several pots or a tray.

  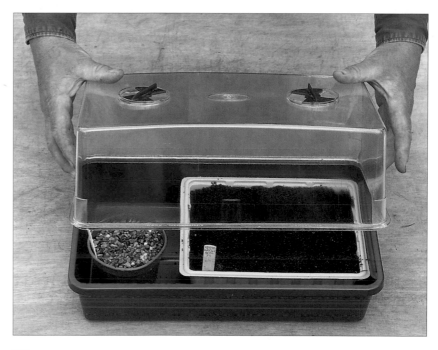

4 Cover the seed with a layer of compost or fine gravel. Gravel will help keep the surface moist, as well as make it easier to water in the seed evenly.

5 Water the pot thoroughly either from above with a watering can or from below by standing the pot in a tray of shallow water.

6 Label the container then place out of direct sunlight. Most seeds do not require heat in order to germinate, but the process can be speeded up if the pots and trays are placed in a propagator.

7 After a few weeks, in some cases only days, the seedlings will appear. Harden them off by gradually removing the lid of the propagator.

Above: *A number of plants such as hellebores* (Helleborus), *will germinate more freely if the seed is fresh, that is as soon as it has ripened, rather than waiting until spring.*

Sowing Annual Seed in Rows

There are several ways to sow annuals. Hardy annuals can be sown directly in the soil, in either spring or autumn. For speed, most half-hardy or tender annuals are sown under glass, but many can also be sown directly in the open soil once the threat of frosts is past.

Above: Dianthus barbatus *'Messenger Mixed', a biennial, can be sown outside in open ground and takes a year to come into flower.*

BIENNIALS

Biennials such as wallflowers (*Erysimum*) or sweet Williams (*Dianthus barbatus*) are the types of plant that are most frequently sown outside in rows, in a spare piece of ground, rather than in the positions where they are intended to flower. Since they take a year to come into flower, it is not usually desirable for them to take up valuable bedding or border space during their growing stage when, visually, not much is happening. It is therefore a good idea to find some space for them in the vegetable garden or in specially allocated nursery beds. They are sown in the spring then planted in their flowering positions in the autumn, after the current year's annuals have finished flowering and been cleared away.

SOWING

Before you begin sowing, you need to prepare the ground thoroughly. Remove all the perennial weeds, preferably during the autumn before sowing so that the soil can lie fallow during the winter.

In the spring, break the soil down into a fine tilth. Using a garden line and a hoe draw out a shallow drill in the soil. If there has not been much rain, the soil will be dry. So, water along the drill (alternatively, you can water after the drill has been raked over) and then sow the seed thinly. Rake the soil back over the seed. Mark the row with two sticks, one at each end, and a label. This is important because you will be surprised how quickly you forget what you have planted which will make it difficult to plan planting schemes when you eventually transplant the seedlings.

When the seedlings have germinated, thin out the plants to 10–15cm (4–6in) apart. Keep them weed-free, and water during dry spells. In the autumn, move the plants to their flowering positions, having first rejuvenated the soil by removing weeds and digging it over, adding plenty of well-rotted organic material.

As well as biennials, annuals for cutting and spare plants to use as replacements in bedding schemes or containers can be grown in this way. The advantage of sowing hardy annuals in the autumn is that they are already in flower at the time the spring-sown ones are being planted out. Combined with the spring-sown plants they create a longer flowering season.

Above: *Pot marigolds* (Calendula officinalis*) come into flower much earlier if they are sown in the open ground during the autumn.*

SOWING IN ROWS

1 Prepare the ground thoroughly, digging it over and breaking it down into a fine tilth using a rake. Do not work the soil when it is too wet or it will become compacted.

2 Using a garden line as a guide, draw out a shallow drill. Use the corner of a hoe, a stick or a trowel.

ANNUALS FOR AUTUMN SOWING

Agrostemma githago (corn cockle)
Calendula officinalis (pot marigold)
Centaurea cyanus (cornflower)
Collinsia grandiflora
Consolida ambigua, syn. *C. ajacis* (larkspur)
Eschscholzia californica
Gypsophila elegans
Iberis umbellata
Lathyrus odoratus (sweet pea)
Limnanthes douglasii (poached-egg plant)
Myosotis (forget-me-not)
Nigella damascena (love-in-a-mist)
Papaver rhoeas (field poppy)
Scabiosa atropurpurea (sweet scabious)

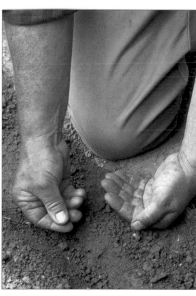

3 If the soil is very dry, water the drill using a watering can and leave to drain. It should not be muddy for sowing.

4 Identify the row with a clearly labelled marker. This is especially important because when the row is backfilled it will be impossible to see where the seed is until it germinates.

5 Sow the seed along the drill. Sow thinly to reduce the amount of thinning required.

6 Rake the soil back over the drill and lightly tamp it down with the back of the rake. When the seedlings emerge, thin them out to prevent overcrowding.

Sowing Annual Seed in Situ

Most annuals that are sown directly in the open soil are sown in situ, that is they are sown where they are to flower. This method is usually used for plants that are going to flower in drifts or blocks rather than intricate patterns. It can be used for autumn-sown plants but it is more usually used for seed sown after the frosts have passed in late spring. By then the soil has warmed up and usually annuals germinate very quickly and soon reach flowering size.

PREPARING THE GROUND

Prepare the ground well, preferably in autumn, removing all weeds and breaking it down to a fine tilth. In some cases the planting will be among perennials or some other permanent planting, and so the area will already be defined, but if it is a large bed broken up into several different blocks or areas, then some pre-planning will be required.

Work out on paper the shapes and locations of the various blocks or drifts of plants. The design can be precise or rough, depending on the accuracy you want to achieve. Transfer this outline to the ground by trailing sand, from either your hand or a bottle, around each area. For precise marking, first draw a grid over the design on paper then create an equivalent grid on the bed using canes and string. Using the grids as guides, transfer the design exactly on to the ground.

SOWING

Once the area has been marked out to your satisfaction, the seed can be sown. There are two methods. The first is to broadcast the seed over the allocated space, simply by taking a handful of seed and scattering it evenly over the soil. The second is to draw out short parallel rows, not too far apart, across the area and sow into these. The first is quicker and creates a natural looking effect, but broadcasting evenly can be difficult and there may be bald areas. The second takes more time but ensures a more even coverage, and also makes weeding easier as you can hoe between rows. Although sown in rows, a random look can be achieved by careful thinning.

If you want the various blocks to merge, scatter a little of the seed into the next area so that the line between adjacent plantings becomes blurred once the plants have matured.

THINNING

Unless you have sown the seed very thinly, you will need to thin out the plants once they have germinated. If you are planning a formal bedding scheme then thin out at regular distances, to create a pattern. Alternatively, for a more natural look, thin at random intervals. If the seed was sown in rows, removing plants at irregular intervals will help break up the lines. Replant a few if necessary to create a still more random effect.

SOWING SEED IN DRIFTS

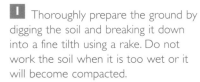 **1** Thoroughly prepare the ground by digging the soil and breaking it down into a fine tilth using a rake. Do not work the soil when it is too wet or it will become compacted.

2 If you are planning to use several different blocks of plants, mark out the design on the soil using contrasting coloured sand or compost (soil mix).

3 Broadcast the seed by hand so that it is thinly spread right across the appropriate area. It will probably be necessary to thin out the seedlings when they appear.

4 Gently rake the seed in so that it is covered by a thin layer of soil.

5 Some gardeners prefer to sow in short rows rather than broadcasting. This makes it easier to weed when the seed first comes up. Draw out shallow drills with a hoe.

6 Sow the seed thinly along each row and rake the soil back over them. By carefully thinning the seedlings the resulting overall pattern of the plants will appear to be random and not in rows.

7 Finally, gently water the whole bed, using a watering can fitted with a fine rose.

8 A bed planted with annuals begins to fill out soon after sowing and planting.

Above: *This delightful annual relative of the delphinium,* Consolida ambigua, *can be sown directly into the open border.*

Pricking Out and Hardening Off

Seed that is germinated in pots needs to be pricked out, which simply means that the seedlings are potted up separately. Perennials are nearly always pricked out into individual pots, whilst annuals, because of their quantities, may demand a half-tray or tray.

THE RIGHT TIME

Seedlings are ready to prick out when they have developed the first true leaves (the first pair of leaves are known as the seed leaves; the second pair are known as the first true leaves) or when the seedlings are large enough to handle. Knock the rootball of seedlings from the pot and gently break it apart so that the seedlings can be easily separated out. Fill a 9cm (3½in) pot with good quality potting compost (soil mix) and make a hole in the centre of the pot with your finger.

Pick up a seedling, holding on to a lower leaf (never touch the roots), and suspend it in the hole in the compost (soil mix). You should be able to see where the soil level had been when it was in its seed pot by the mark on the stem. Line up this mark with the compost (soil mix) level in the pot and, with your other hand, trickle more compost (soil mix) around the roots. When the hole is full, tap the pot on the bench and gently firm down. It is a good idea to label each of the pots with the name of the seedling and the sowing date. Water the seedling from below by standing the pot in a shallow tray of water or from above with a fine-rosed watering can.

To ensure that the seedling will recover from the shock of being transplanted and start growing away, the pot should be stood in a closed cold frame, or, alternatively, kept in a draught-free place in a greenhouse. Once you are certain that the plant has become established, it can be hardened off by gradually opening the cold frame over a period of a week to two weeks, until eventually the lid is left open all the time. If the plants are kept in a greenhouse, they can be set outside for increasing lengths of time over a similar period.

Once the plants have been hardened off, they can either be planted in their permanent positions in the border, or they can be left standing in an open cold frame. An alternative solution is to make a plunge bed. This is a simple frame with no lid, built from wooden planks, bricks or blocks. It is part-filled with sand or ashes and the pots are stood on or partially plungéd into this mixture. The plunge bed helps to keep the roots cool in the summer and warm in the winter, as well as providing a small amount of moisture through the drainage holes in the bases of the pots.

PRICKING OUT SEEDLINGS

1 As soon as seedlings are large enough, they should be pricked out. Water the pot an hour or so before gently knocking out the seedlings.

2 Gently break up the rootball, finding a natural dividing line between plants. Split into clumps, dealing with one at a time.

3 Gently ease the seedlings away from each clump, one at a time. Only touch the leaves, not the roots or stems.

4 Hold the seedling over a pot by one or more of its seed leaves and gently trickle compost (soil mix) around its roots until the pot is full.

5 Tap the pot on the bench to settle the compost (soil mix) and then gently firm down with your thumbs. Add some more compost (soil mix) if necessary.

6 Water the pots with a watering can or stand them in a tray of water. Keep the plants covered in a cold frame for a day or so, before hardening them off.

Above: *Yellow-flowered* Verbascum olympicum *and hollyhocks* (Alcea rosea) *make a striking planting combination*.

Buying Plants

Growing plants from seeds or cuttings is a rewarding part of gardening, but some gardeners prefer to obtain their plants ready grown. This may be because they have not got the facilities or the time, or simply because growing everything from seed or cuttings does not appeal to them. The easy option is to buy young plants from a garden centre or nursery.

ADVANTAGES AND DISADVANTAGES

There are advantages and disadvantages to buying plants rather than growing them yourself. The main advantage is the convenience of buying plants that are usually ready to plant out. If you have set your heart on a particular plant that you want for your garden now, you may not want to wait while it grows from seed, particularly in the case of a biennial. An established specimen can make an immediate impact in a bed or border.

The main disadvantage is that your choice may be restricted. The choice offered in a seed merchant's catalogue will always be much wider than is available in plants at a garden centre or nursery. Very often you will find that colour choice is restricted. For example, the annual snapdragons (*Antirrhinum*) may be offered as seed in a whole range of single colours, as well as tall or short plants, or even different types of flower. If you buy annuals such as these as plants, you may be offered only trays of mixed colours with no other options.

A wider selection of plants is available if you buy through mail order, and increasing numbers of reputable nurseries are providing this service. Order well in advance because plants sell out. If you are likely to be away when the plants arrive, give the nursery a suitable date so that it does not dispatch the plants before you are ready to deal with them. A parcel of plants that has been sitting on a doorstep in full sun is a sorry sight indeed.

As soon as the plants have been delivered, put them into a cool greenhouse or other sheltered place, out of the sun, in order to allow them to recover. If necessary, pot them on before eventually hardening them off and planting them out.

QUALITY

If you want good-quality plants that are accurately labelled, it is essential to go to a reputable source. Many roadside nurseries and market stalls that sell just a few plants may offer good bargains, but the plants may not always be labelled correctly. If you buy plants that are already in flower, then of course you can be sure of their identity, otherwise you may choose to risk being surprised when the flowers come out – differently to how you expected.

Above: *A group of foxgloves makes a dramatic impact against a background of silver foliage.*

TIPS ON BUYING PLANTS

1 Most plants are now sold in pots, although annual bedding plants tend to be sold in cells or strips because of the quantities needed.

2 Although this can be tricky in a garden centre, it is advisable to see if the plant is pot-bound. A plant such as the one on the left will have great difficulty in spreading its roots and growing properly.

3 Buying annuals in strips is a popular method of obtaining large numbers of plants at low cost. Young plants have plenty of room to develop a good root system.

4 Traditionally, perennials were bought bare-rooted, having been grown in the ground and dug up when needed. Bare-rooted plants should be bought only between late autumn and early spring.

Containers

These days most plants are sold in containers and are available all year round. In the past, and still occasionally today, plants were sold bare-rooted, usually wrapped in hessian; such plants should only be bought between late autumn and early spring.

Annuals and perennials are sold in a range of different containers. Individual pots are the best because plants have room to develop in them, but they are liable to be more expensive. Bedding plants are frequently sold in cells or strips; these are much cheaper, and as long as the plants are not too old or crowded, they should prove satisfactory. Always check your prospective purchase carefully and reject any plant that is diseased, or looks drawn. If possible, knock it out of its pot and look at the roots. Again, reject any that are pot-bound, that is, the roots are wound round and round inside the pot creating a solid mass. Such plants can be very difficult to establish, but if you have no option, you can increase their chances of sucess by gently teasing out the roots before planting them.

When choosing plants, large, well-grown specimens are obviously preferable, but health and vigour are more important than size. If the plant in question is in flower, you have the added advantage of seeing exactly what colour they are, but do choose one with plenty of buds rather than one which may be almost past its best. If the plants for sale are in a greenhouse or tunnel, harden them off as soon as you get home. Planting them straight into the garden may put them under stress, from which they might not recover.

A wider selection of plants is available if you buy through mail order, and increasing numbers of reputable nurseries are providing this valuable service. Once you have selected the plants you wish to buy, always ensure that you order them well in advance because plants are likely to sell out.

If you are likely to be away when the plants arrive, give the nursery a suitable date for delivery, so that they do not dispatch the plants before you are ready to deal with them. A parcel of plants that has been sitting on a doorstep in full sun is a very sorry sight indeed.

Both annuals and perennials purchased by mail order are liable to come as "plugs", that is individual plantlets either bare-rooted or in cells. As soon as the plants have been delivered, put them into a cool greenhouse or other sheltered place, out of the sun, in order to allow them to recover. If necessary, pot these up and grow them on for a bit longer before planting out.

Above: *A combination of trailing petunias with busy Lizzies and pelargoniums makes a lovely hanging basket in fresh, sunny colours.*

Some of the best plants come in individual pots, but they are much more expensive to buy as more work and attention were required to raise them. The plants have more compost (soil mix) in which to grow and can be left in them longer.

In packs of plugs, young plants are grown in small cells. These are cheaper than those in larger packs, but make sure they have not become pot-bound, starved and drawn through being left too long in the cells.

Planting Out

Planting up a new bed is one of the most exciting tasks that a gardener can perform. There is a real sense of achievement when it is done and a feeling of pride when the bed or border reaches maturity. That the planting never works out quite as one had imagined – sometimes better, sometimes worse – is irrelevant.

PLANNING THE PLANTING

Some gardeners like to pitch straight in with a collection of plants. Others are more cautious and think about the arrangement for a while before they begin planting. While the impulse method may sometimes work, it usually pays to give some thought to how you want your garden to look and what you can do to achieve your wishes.

POINTS TO CONSIDER

The first step is to plan the border or bed. No matter how badly you think you draw, it is always worth trying to sketch out the arrangement of the plants, and at this stage there are several factors to take into consideration. The first important point to consider is, of course, the colour scheme. You should ensure that plants of sympathetic colours are placed together and obvious clashes are avoided. Then there is the question of height. In general, you will want the tallest plants at the back and the shortest ones at the front, but sometimes it is a good idea to add variety by bringing a few of the taller plants forwards. Use your perennials to provide the basic framework of your border, and leave plenty of gaps for annuals to fill during summer and early autumn.

One of the other points to bear in mind when planning the design of a bed is seasonal changes. Since not all plants bloom at the same time, it is advisable to research the flowering times of your chosen perennials in order to spread the flowering from spring through to the autumn, and include winter, too, if necessary. Make sure that any large areas in the beds or borders that are going to be blank during any of the main seasons are filled with eye-catching annuals in summer and autumn and bulbs in winter and spring.

Also consider the question of fragrance. Plants that benefit

Left: *The combination of hot, vibrant colours, such as rich crimson, deep purple and sunshine yellow, creates a great deal of impact in this border.*

from being smelt close to, or whose leaves give off a fragrance when they are touched, should be planted near the front of the bed, where they will be accessible.

BUYING THE PLANTS

When you have drawn up the planting plan, try to acquire all the plants before you start planting out. It never seems as satisfactory to plant in batches, because the gaps you leave usually turn out to be either too big or too small. Buy or propagate the plants that you need and then grow them on in their pots, either in a cold frame or plunge bed, until they are needed.

PREPARING THE GROUND

The ground should have been prepared some months earlier to allow it to settle down. Break down any remaining large clods in order to form a fine tilth. Dig out any perennial weeds that have appeared and make sure that you remove every piece of root. The best time to do this is in the spring or autumn, although spring is usually preferable, especially on cold, wet soils. Never work when the soil is wet. Wait until the soil is dry enough for you to walk about and work on it without compacting it. If you have to get on a border when the soil is still rather wet, stand on a wooden plank which serves to spread the load.

If your planting plan is complicated, use string and canes to create a grid over the bed or border. Drawing a similar grid on the plan will help you put the plants in their required positions. Another possibility is to mark the soil by drawing lines on it with sand or peat, which

can be trickled through your fingers or put into an empty bottle and poured out in a steady stream as you move around the outlines.

PUTTING IN THE PLANTS

Put all the plants, still in their pots, in their planting positions. Stand back and walk around the border, assessing the effect and trying to visualize the final result. Some plants will need to be moved because of colour clashes or for other reasons. Others will be too close when they are mature and will need to be moved. A few minutes spent doing this, before you begin to plant, will be time well spent if it avoids you having to transplant something that has grown too large for its position.

When you are satisfied with the positions of all the plants, you can begin to plant. Start at the back and move forwards, making sure that the plants are put into the soil at the same depth as they were in their pots. Water in each plant thoroughly, and then rake through the soil to tidy it up as well as to remove any compaction that has resulted from you having to stand on the soil.

It is rare that everything goes right the first time. There is always at least one plant that is not quite the colour you thought it was going to be and clashes with its neighbours, or one that normally grows to only about 30cm (12in), but enjoys the conditions you have provided so much that it grows to 60cm (2ft) and is in the wrong position.

Some perennials languish and never really settle down. It may be necessary to move these, perhaps replacing them with other plants or just moving

everything around. This is best done in the autumn or in early spring. Dig up the plants with plenty of soil around their roots and, after transplanting, water them in well. You will often find that plants that were unhappy in one particular position will flourish when they are moved

Above: *Newly planted borders grow away surprisingly quickly.*

only a short distance away. The reason for this is often difficult to determine, but there may well have been something in the soil at their first position that disagreed with them.

PLANTING A BED

1 If the bed was dug in the autumn, winter weather should have broken down the soil. In spring, rake over the soil and remove any weeds that have reappeared.

2 Although well-rotted organic material should have been added at the time of digging, a sprinkling of bonemeal will ensure the plants get off to a good start.

3 Draw a grid on a planting plan and then mark out a scaled-up version on the bed, using sand or compost (soil mix). Alternatively, use string stretched between canes to mark out the planting plan.

4 Using your planting plan and grid as a guide, lay out the plants, still in their pots, on the ground. Stand back, and try to envisage the border as it will be, and make any necessary adjustments. Remember to use your annuals as fillers between the perennials.

5 Dig a hole with a trowel or spade and, with the plant still in its pot, check that the depth and width is right. Adjust if necessary.

6 Remove the plant from the pot and place in the planting hole. Fill in the hole with soil and then firm the plant in.

7 When the bed is completely planted, water in all the plants. They should be kept watered until they have become established.

8 Go over the border with a fork, or use a rake if there is room. This will loosen any compacted areas, as well as levelling the soil.

9 Cover the soil between the plants with a layer of mulch, like composted bark, to keep weeds down and preserve moisture.

10 If you are concerned that you will not remember what the plants are, mark each one with a plastic label.

11 The finished border should need little attention, apart from occasionally removing the odd weed.

Watering and Feeding

Compared with other gardening jobs, watering is generally not an onerous task, and feeding, too, is rarely much of a problem, as long as the ground has been prepared well in the first place. The key to watering is to make sure that the ground contains plenty of well-rotted humus. This fibrous material holds moisture but does not cause the ground to become water-logged.

THE IMPORTANCE OF HUMUS

If humus is dug into the soil, it will hold the moisture down at root level, where it is needed. Spreading more organic material over the surface of the soil will help to prevent evaporation and thus also reduce the need to water. Black polythene (plastic) can also be used as a mulch, but looks ugly and is best covered with another mulch such as chipped bark. Farmyard manure, garden compost, chipped or composted bark and spent mushroom compost are among the best forms of mulch. If humus is dug in and the soil is given a top-dressing, there will be little need to water even in dry weather.

WATERING METHODS

Sandy soil does not retain moisture, and it may be necessary to water in dry spells. A sprinkler of some sort is undoubtedly the most effective method for a border. A dribble hose can also be used. This is a hosepipe with a series of evenly spaced holes in it that slowly releases water. It can be buried beneath the mulch. In a wide border you would need lots of pipes to make sure that all plants receive the water they need. If individual plants begin to flag, a watering can is usually sufficient.

Whatever method you decide to use, always make sure that the ground is thoroughly soaked. If you only wet the surface, you will actually do more harm than good as the plants will tend to form shallow roots, rather than seeking water from deep in the soil. Put a rain gauge or a jam jar within the range of the sprinkler, and leave the sprinkler running until there is a reading of at least 2.5cm (1in) of water.

WHEN TO FEED

The same principles hold true for feeding. If the ground is thoroughly prepared in the first place, and then top-dressed with organic material, sufficient nutrients should be available to the plants, and there should be no need for further feeding. Remember that the organic material should be well rotted before it is added to the border, otherwise, in the process of breaking down, it will extract nitrogen from the soil.

Some gardeners who do not have access to much organic material also apply a light feed of a general, balanced fertilizer in spring, but unless your plants are looking particularly starved, there is no need to give them a liquid feed.

1 If they are prepared properly, most borders do not need watering, but in really dry periods a sprinkler is an effective way of covering a large area. Ensure that the ground is thoroughly soaked.

2 Containers are best watered by hand with a watering can. Again, be certain to give the pot a good soaking.

3 Sometimes it is necessary to pep up a flagging border towards the end of a long season. A liquid feed added to a watering can is a quick way to do this. Follow the instructions given by the manufacturer on the bottle.

4 Watering with a hand held hose is time consuming, but several manufacturers make fertilizer dispensers that can be fitted to a hosepipe – this is an easy way to supply feed.

5 Early in the season, if insufficient organic material has been used to top-dress the border, a sprinkling of a general fertilizer will help keep the plants in good condition.

Above: *If a border is fed and mulched in spring and autumn, it should not need further watering, except in very dry conditions.*

Weed Control

One of the least attractive chores associated with any garden plant is keeping it free of weeds, but as long as you keep on top of it, weeding can be a relaxing and even enjoyable pastime. While weeding, you are closer to the plants than you would be simply strolling past, so it is hardly surprising that this is when you will often notice detail in the flowers and foliage that you would normally miss. It also gives you the opportunity to check that each plant is healthy and not suffering from any pest or disease.

WEEDING

The secret of successful weeding is thorough ground preparation before you sow or plant and then to keep on top of the weeding by doing it regularly. Once you lose control of the weeds in a bed, they begin to take over, after which weeding becomes an uphill battle.

Never plant a bed that has weeds already in it. Clear it thoroughly first. Once you have planted, hoe between the plants regularly to kill any newly germinated weeds. Once the plants begin to fill out, hoeing might damage plants accidentally so you will have to resort to hand-weeding. However, by this stage there should be few weeds and you just need to keep an eye out for the odd weed and pull it out before it can become too large or start spreading.

MULCHES

You can cut down considerably on the labour of weeding by preventing weed seeds from germinating, and a mulch is an effective way to achieve this,

though it will not stop perennial weeds. A mulch is a layer of well-rotted organic material, chipped bark or a similar material, that is placed on the surface of the soil. When applying a mulch, always water first, then cover the soil with a 10cm (4in) layer.

Peat does not have much value as a mulch because it will blow away as soon as it dries out and it adds very little to the soil as it breaks down. Straw and grass cuttings can be used but they are extremely ugly and are best reserved for the back of beds where they are hidden from view by tall plants. Farmyard manure is good but quality varies and frequently it is full of weed seed just waiting to germinate.

HERBICIDES

Try to avoid using too many chemicals in the garden. It may be necessary, especially on heavy soils, to use herbicides to clear the ground initially, but after planting they are best avoided, as they are likely to damage adjacent plants.

1 Weeds should be eradicated for several reasons: they make a bed look untidy; they use up a great deal of moisture and nutrients; many harbour pests and diseases.

2 Where plants are close together, the best way of removing weeds is either to pull them out by hand or to dig them out using a hand fork. Perennial weeds must be dug out whole and not simply chopped off, or they will soon return.

3 Where there is more room, hoes can be used in a border, but take care to avoid your precious plants. In hot weather hoed-up weeds can be left to shrivel, but it looks much neater if they are all removed to the compost heap.

4 After weeding, rake through the border with a fork or, if the plants are far enough apart, with a rake. This will tidy up the bed and level off the surface, removing any footprints and any weed remnants.

Below: *This well-tended border is an excellent example of one in which the weeds are kept at bay partly by weeding and partly by close planting. This technique means that the weeds cannot become established.*

5 It is a good idea to apply or renew a mulch after weeding. As well as helping to prevent weeds from reappearing, this will also preserve moisture. Composted or chipped bark will set the plants off well.

Staking

One important procedure that should not be neglected, both for the look of the border and the health of the plants, is staking. There are two important factors to remember: make the stakes discreet, so that they are as invisible as possible, and do stake early, before the plants flop.

PLANTS THAT NEED STAKING

Most gardeners find that at least one plant is blown over at some time during the year, and even in sheltered areas, where there is little or no wind, a heavy downpour of rain can cause problems, especially with double flowers, which tend to hold water. Double peonies, for example, have heavy flower-heads, which will often bow down under their own weight. When they are full of rainwater, they topple over as if they were filled with lead.

The key to solving these problems, as with so many aspects of gardening, is to anticipate possible trouble and to stake vulnerable plants before they are big enough to pose a problem. Once a plant has fallen over, it is impossible to stake it in a way that will make it look natural. Plants should always be staked before they are fully grown. This not only affords the plant protection before it is likely to need it, but also allows the plant to grow over its support so that this cannot be seen. Most plants need support between a half and two-thirds of the way up their eventual height, which means that the supports should be in position before the plant reaches half its height. The plant will then be able to grow through the framework.

USING PEA-STICKS

The best staking methods are those that provide some form of lattice through which the plant can grow. One of the most satisfactory methods is to use pea-sticks or brushwood, if available. These twiggy branches are pushed into the ground, right up against the plant. The top twigs are then bent over and interlaced or tied to form a grid through which the growing stems can pass. As the plant grows through the top and sides of this framework, its leaves will cover it, and will eventually hide it completely.

MAKING A CAT'S CRADLE

A similar method is to insert small stakes or canes in the ground and then weave a random cat's cradle of string around them. A more technical method, but one that has the same result, is to use ready-made hoops that have grids of wire welded across them. These are supported on sturdy wire legs at the appropriate height.

Left: *This garden displays a variety of different ways in which plants can be provided with support, including the use of large-mesh wire netting, pea-sticks, and a frame for climbing plants.*

MAKING A CAT'S CRADLE

1 A cheap but effective means of support can be created by forming a cat's cradle of canes and string. Push the canes into the soil around and in the middle of the clumps of plants that need to be supported.

2 Trim off the tops of the canes, so that they will not show above the plants when they are fully grown.

For large areas of plants a similar device can be made by supporting a sheet of large-mesh wire netting horizontally above the plants. The netting can be held in place quite easily, using a series of stakes or canes.

Interlocking stakes, which you should be able to find in most garden centres as well as in many hardware stores, can be placed in any shape, whether regular or irregular, around a clump of plants. A few of these stakes can also be placed horizontally in order to create a grid. They can also be used in a line to provide support for plants that otherwise would flop over a path or lawn. If you do find that you have neglected to stake your plants in time, then these stakes are the best way to lift plants back up again.

STAKING SINGLE PLANTS

All the methods described so far are for supporting clumps of plants. But some tall border plants – delphiniums and hollyhocks, for example – consist of one or a series of vulnerable spikes. These can be staked individually with long canes. If possible, place the cane behind the stem so that it is not so obvious when you are viewing the border. It is rarely necessary for the cane to be as tall as the stem, and a flower stem attached all the way up a tall cane will appear stiff and rigid, giving the plant an artificial look. A better approach is to support the lower part of the stem, allowing the top to move freely. In this way the stake will be less obtrusive, and the plant will appear more natural.

3 Weave string in a random pattern between all the canes so that a mesh of supports is created. At the end of the season, remove the supports from the plants.

A SELECTION OF STAKING METHODS

1 Proprietary hoops with adjustable legs can be placed over the plants. The plants grow through the grid, gaining support from the frame, and eventually hiding it. altogether.

2 A good method for supporting clumps of varying sizes and shapes is to use linked stakes that are simply slotted together. These stakes are particularly good for rescuing plants that have flopped over.

USING PEA-STICKS

5 Tall flowering stems can be staked individually by tying them to a cane that is shorter than the eventual height of the plant and hidden from sight behind the stem.

1 Pea-sticks are a cheap, renewable form of support. Push the sticks into the ground around the perimeter of the plants.

3 For larger areas of plants, a sheet of large-mesh wire netting can be supported horizontally over the plants by tying it to wooden posts or canes.

4 Wire netting can also be used vertically to create cylinders, which are held firmly in place with posts. The plant grows up through the centre, with the leaves and branches coming through and covering the sides.

2 Bend over the tops of the sticks at what will be about two-thirds of the eventual height of the plants. Twine and tie the tips together to form a mesh.

3 For climbing plants, such as *Lathyrus*, a tall pyramid of pea-sticks can be created. This will be hidden when the plant attains full growth.

Autumn and Winter Maintenance

A few hours spent working on a border in winter will save many hours the following year. There are a surprising number of autumn and winter days when the soil is sufficiently dry and the weather pleasant enough to get out into the garden and do some work, and you should take advantage of those days whenever you can.

WHEN TO TIDY

Some gardeners like to leave all the work in the garden until spring, and they usually cite two reasons for so doing. The first is that the dead stems can look attractive in the winter; the second is that they provide food and shelter for birds, insects and small mammals. Both points are undoubtedly true, but the rush to get everything done at the start of the year can be something of a nightmare, especially if the spring is wet. When plants have started into growth before you have had time to tackle them, trying to cut back dead stems without damaging the new shoots is far from easy.

On the other hand, if you work steadily through the winter months, not only will you be ahead of the game, you will also save yourself a great deal of work later on. Weeding in the winter means that you have more time to sit and enjoy the garden in the summer.

REMOVING OLD GROWTH

One of the major jobs in the perennial garden is cutting down and removing the old stems from the previous year's plants. These should be cut off as low to the ground as possible with a pair of secateurs (pruners). Rather than burning or throwing away this material, compost it, shredding it first if it is woody, and return it to the soil once it has rotted down. You will need to prune the live growth of some plants, rather than simply cutting off the dead growth. Many of these – artemisias and penstemons, for example – are best left until spring.

WEEDING

Once you can see the ground, the next task is to remove any weeds. Avoid using a hoe because you may accidentally damage shoots that are just below the surface. Weed by hand, using a hand or border fork. When the border is clean, lightly dig between the plants, but avoid getting too close to them, especially those with spreading, shallow roots. Cover the whole border with a layer of well-rotted organic material, such as farmyard manure.

While you are working through the border, take the opportunity to divide any plants that are becoming too congested. Dig them out, divide them and replant them after having taken the opportunity to rejuvenate the soil by digging it over and incorporating humus as you work.

MAINTENANCE TASKS

1 It might seem like an impossible task to turn the overgrown mess shown above into an attractive border, but, if you work steadily throughout the winter, the border will be transformed.

2 Carefully cut back all dead stems as close to the ground as possible. As winter passes, more shoots will appear at the base and care will be needed not to damage them.

3 Some herbaceous plants remain green throughout winter. Cut back to sound growth, removing dead and leggy material.

4 Here, the old stems have been cut off so that they are level with the emerging growth, so as not to damage it.

5 Lightly dig over the soil around the plants, removing any weeds. Avoid digging around plants such as asters which have shallow roots.

6 Top-dress around the plants with some organic material, such as well-rotted compost, farmyard manure or composted bark. Avoid using peat.

7 Some plants need some form of winter protection. Here, the crowns of some gunneras have been covered with their own leaves from the previous season.

Dealing with Pests and Diseases

In a well-managed garden, pests and diseases should not be too much of a problem. Growing a variety of plants, keeping a watchful eye and good hygiene are the key notes.

THE BENEFITS OF VARIETY

The greater the variety of plants you grow in the garden, the fewer pests and diseases you are likely to encounter, because the greatest problems come with monocultures. If you grow only roses, for example, there is lots of food for aphids, and once they start breeding they spread very rapidly and become almost uncontrollable. Unfortunately, roses are not a home for the ladybirds and hoverflies that prey on aphids, so you may have to resort to chemical controls. In a mixed herbaceous border, not only is the number of plants that will be attacked by aphids limited, but there are also plenty of host plants for their predators, and so a balance is struck and the gardener rarely has to interfere.

Another advantage of the mixed border is that if one plant falls prey to a particular insect or disease, it is probable that its neighbours will not succumb. When blackspot sweeps through a rose garden, however, all the plants are likely to be affected. Thus, diversity in a garden helps enormously to control both the incidence and effects of pests.

KEEPING THE GARDEN TIDY

Good gardening involves keeping tidy the garden, in general, and the borders, in particular. Clearing away dead leaves and dying material will remove the homes and food for many pests and diseases. Compost this type of material before returning it to the border. However, if the leaves are under a plant that has had a fungal disease or if the stems are the remains of such a plant, you should not only remove them but destroy them as well to help reduce the number of spores that can attack again.

Many weeds are hosts to diseases, especially fungal ones – groundsel, for example, is often infected with a rust, that can be transmitted to hollyhocks and other plants. Weeding not only removes the source of disease, but gives you an opportunity to examine the plants in the border. An outbreak of greenfly can be easily checked if you remove the advance guard with your fingers.

If pests and diseases do gain hold it may be necessary to apply chemical controls, but these are rarely necessary in a well-maintained garden. If you need to spray, always follow the instructions on the packet and only spray those areas affected by the pest; do not drench everything in sight.

Slugs can be one of the worst pests that the gardener is likely to meet. You can use bait if you prefer, but going out over several consecutive nights and rounding them up by torchlight usually brings the situation under control.

1 A variety of methods can be used to combat pests and diseases, including netting and black thread to keep off or deter birds and mammals, baits for slugs and snails, puffer packs of chemical dust as well as liquid sprays for insect pests and fungal diseases.

2 Slugs and snails are two of the gardener's worst enemies, particularly in late winter and early spring when new growth can be reduced so much that plants fail to grow. Removing these pests by hand at night is one of the most effective methods of control.

3 Butterfly and moth caterpillars can cause a lot of damage to both flowers and foliage. You can usually maintain sufficient control over the problem by picking the caterpillars off by hand. If necessary, there is a range of sprays and dusts available that can be used instead.

4 Fungal diseases, such as the mildew shown here, are often a problem, especially in either very dry or very wet years. Asters are particularly prone to mildew. Thinning the plants to improve air circulation may help, or you can spray with either a chemical or an organic fungicide.

5 The damage done by rabbits and other mammals can be heartbreaking because they will often browse a plant to the ground. The best form of defence is to surround the garden with a wire netting fence.

6 Although aphids, such as greenfly and blackfly, are among the most common of insect pests, a mixed garden usually attracts enough predators to keep them under control. When serious outbreaks occur, chemical control may be the only solution.

Pinching Out, Dead-heading and Trimming

Many plants have a long flowering season, often extending from early summer into the autumn and sometimes beyond. Needless to say, they will need a little bit of attention from time to time in order to keep them looking neat.

PINCHING OUT

If left to their own devices, many plants will grow only one main stem. In a bedding scheme, for example, this would result in a forest of tall spindly spikes with large gaps in between them, rather than a desirable carpet of flowers and foliage. To avoid this effect, pinch out the growing tip of each main spike. This will cause the stem to produce side shoots, which will make the plants much more bushy. Further pinching out will increase the effect.

DEAD-HEADING

As the season progresses, flowers appear, then die, once they have been pollinated and have served their purpose. The petals go brown and look ugly, spoiling the effect of the still perfect flowers around them. Regular dead-heading keeps everything neat and tidy and looking in much better condition.

Another good reason for regular dead-heading is to prevent seed formation. Producing seed is the natural goal of every plant, and once they have been pollinated, they direct all their energy into forming the seeds, then die (in the case of annuals) or die back (in the case of perennials). If their fading flowers are removed, they will redirect their energy into producing more flowers.

TRIMMING BACK

New flowers are normally produced towards the tips of shoots, so as the flowering season progresses and more and more flowers are produced, the stems get longer and longer. Before too long the plants begin to look somewhat straggly. Cut these stems back every so often so that new shoots are formed, keeping the plant compact. You can do this all at once, but the plant may take a while to recover its flowering habit, so it is preferable to cut off a few at a time to prevent any interruption in flowering.

TOOLS

Secateurs (pruners) are the most versatile of tools, especially those that have pointed jaws so that you can get right into the leaf joints. Strong pointed scissors are also useful, especially for small plants. Knives can be used in most situations, as long as they are sharp. Many stems can be snapped or pinched out with the fingers or fingernails, but make certain that the action is clean-cut and does not bruise the stem.

1 Many plants will grow up as a single stem, making rather spindly growth. However, if the tip is pinched out, side shoots will develop and the plant will become completely bushy and much more attractive. Cut through the stem with secateurs (pruners) or a knife, just above a leaf joint.

2 The pinched-out plants fill out, creating a solid mass of attractive foliage. Planted together, they make an attractive mass planting.

DEAD-HEADING

1 Dead heads left on plants, especially light-coloured flowers as seen here, look very scruffy if they are not removed regularly. Another good reason for dead-heading is to redirect the plant's energy that would normally go into seed production into producing new flowers, so prolonging the flowering season.

2 Using scissors, a sharp knife or secateurs (pruners), snip off the flowers neatly and cleanly where they join the stem. Sometimes the whole head of flowers needs to be removed, in which case cut these back to the first set of leaves. Dead flower heads and other clippings can be added to the compost heap.

3 Regular and carefully executed dead-heading produces a much cleaner and healthier looking arrangement. It takes only a short time and the effort is worthwhile.

TIDYING UP

1 Some edging plants spread out over the grass, possibly killing it or creating bald patches, as has this poached egg plant (Limnanthes douglasii).

2 If the plant has finished flowering, as here, it can be removed completely. Otherwise, just cut back the part that is encroaching on grass. On a brick or stone path, there may be no problem, though it could still cause people to stumble.

Taking Stem Cuttings

Increasing perennial plants by cuttings is an easy way to propagate them. If the plant to be increased is a mature specimen, it will usually mean that there is plenty of cutting material, in which case this method can be almost as productive as growing new plants from seed.

SUITABLE PERENNIALS

One of the advantages of increasing plants from cuttings is that the resulting plants are identical to the parent plant. For many plants it is, in fact, the only means of propagation, especially if your chosen plant is a sterile hybrid that does not produce seed and is impossible to divide. Some plants – the wallflower *Erysimum cheiri* 'Harpur Crew' and many of the pinks (*Dianthus*), for example – have continued to be propagated in this way for centuries, and our existing plants are still closely related to the original parents that grew all those years ago. In effect, they still contain part of the original plant.

Not all perennial plants can be propagated from cuttings. Experienced gardeners will often know simply by looking at a plant whether it is possible or not, but the reasons for this are difficult to describe. Most encyclopedias of plants and books on propagation indicate those that can be propagated in this way, so you can consult these, or simply learn by trial and error.

HOW TO TAKE CUTTINGS

Most cuttings are taken in spring and summer, but many plants can be rooted at any time of the year. Penstemons are a good example of this.

The procedure for taking cuttings is straightforward. Pieces of stem are removed from the plant, trimmed up, placed in damp cutting compost (planting mix) and left in a closed environment until they have rooted. The cuttings are then potted up and treated as any other young plants. Stem cuttings can be taken either from the tip of a mature stem or from the new growth at the base of a plant, in which case they are called basal cuttings.

Cuttings taken should generally be about 10cm (4in) long. In most cases it is the top of the stem that is used, but in some cases – penstemons, for example – any part of the stem can be used as long as it is not too woody. Always choose non-flowering shoots or remove any flowerheads.

Once the cutting is removed from the plant, it should be placed in a polythene (plastic) bag to keep it fresh and to prevent wilting. As soon as possible, remove the cuttings one by one from the bag and prepare them by using a sharp knife to cut through the stem just below a leaf node – that is, where a leaf joins the stem.

Most of the leaves should then be neatly trimmed off, tight to the stem, leaving just the top pair or, if they are small, two pairs. The cutting is then placed in a pot of cutting compost (planting mix). It has been found that cuttings root better if they are arranged around the edge of the pot. Several cuttings can be placed in

PERENNIALS FROM STEM TIP CUTTINGS

Argyranthemum frutescens (marguerite)
Cestrum parqui
Clematis
Dianthus (carnations, pinks)
Diascia
Erysimum (wallflower)
Euphorbia (spurge; some)
Gazania (treasure flower)
Geranium (cranesbill; some)
Helichrysum petiolare (liquorice plant)
Lavatera (tree mallow)
Lobelia
Lythrum (purple loosestrife)
Malva (mallow)
Mimulus (monkey flower, musk)
Osteospermum
Parahebe perfoliata
Pelargonium
Penstemon
Phygelius
Salvia (sage)
Sphaeralcea (globe mallow)
Stachys coccinea
Trifolium pratense (red clover)
Verbena
Viola
Vinca (periwinkle)

the same pot – as many as twelve in a 9cm (3½in) pot – as long as they do not touch.

Some gardeners first dip the bottom of the cutting into a hormone rooting powder or liquid, although most perennials will root quite satisfactorily without this. An advantage of rooting compounds is that they usually contain a fungicide, which reduces the risk of rotting. Rooting compounds quickly lose their efficacy, and it is important to buy new stock every year.

Above: *Monkey flowers (*Mimulus*) are among those perennials that can be propagated by taking stem tip cuttings.*

TAKING STEM TIP CUTTINGS

1 Take cuttings from the tips of the stems and put them in a polythene bag. The length of the cuttings will vary, depending on the subject, but take about 10cm (4in).

2 Trim the cuttings to just below a leaf joint, and then remove most of the leaves and side-shoots, leaving just two at the top.

3 Place up to twelve cuttings in a pot of cutting compost (planting mix) or a 50:50 mixture of sharp sand and peat or peat substitute.

4 Water well, and cover the pot with the cut-off base of a soft-drinks bottle. This makes a perfect substitute for a propagator.

5 A heated propagator will speed up the rooting process. Several containers can be placed in the same unit.

AFTERCARE

Once the cuttings have been inserted into the compost (soil mix), label and water the pot, which should then be placed in a propagator or cold frame. A heated propagator, especially one that is heated from the bottom, will speed up the rooting process but it is by no means essential – any closed environment will suffice: you could simply use a polythene (plastic) bag, as long as the cuttings do not touch the sides.

Leave the cuttings in the propagator until they have rooted. This will be evident when roots appear at the drainage holes at the bottom of the pot. At this stage, pot up the cuttings individually and grow them on.

BASAL CUTTINGS

These cuttings are struck in exactly the same way as stem tip cuttings except that they are taken from the new growth at the base of the plant rather than from a mature stem. Although basal cuttings are often taken in the spring, when the plant first gets into growth, they can also be taken at other times of the year, simply by shearing over the plant. This removes all the older growth and encourages new shoots to start from the base. This new growth provides the material for the cuttings.

Taking basal cuttings is a useful method for increasing most asters, as well as violas, anthemis and nepetas. Other perennials that can be increased in this way are achilleas, phlox and dahlias.

TAKING BASAL CUTTINGS

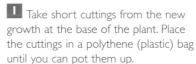 **1** Take short cuttings from the new growth at the base of the plant. Place the cuttings in a polythene (plastic) bag until you can pot them up.

2 Trim the base of the cuttings. Cut through the stem just below a leaf joint and then remove all the leaves, except for a few at the top.

Above: *Lupins (Lupinus), with their racemes of pea-like flowers, can be propagated by taking basal cuttings.*

3 Place the cuttings in a pot of cutting compost (planting mix) made up of 50:50 sharp sand and peat or peat substitute. You can grow up to twelve in a pot.

4 Label the pot so that you will remember what the plants are, as they may all look the same. Also include the date on which you took the cuttings.

5 Water the pot and place it in a propagator. You can use a polythene bag, but ensure that no leaves are touching the polythene. Seal with an elastic band.

6 When the roots of the cuttings appear at the drainage holes of the pot, gently remove the contents.

7 Although this well-rooted cutting is shown here on the hand, it is best to avoid touching young roots if possible.

8 Pot up the rooted cuttings in individual pots, using a good quality potting compost. Keep covered for a few days and then harden off.

PERENNIALS FROM BASAL CUTTINGS

Achillea (yarrow)
Anthemis
Artemisia (wormwood)
Aster (Michaelmas daisy)
Campanula (bellflower)
Chrysanthemum
Crambe
Dahlia
Delphinium
Diascia
Epilobium (willowherb)
Gaillardia (blanket flower)
Helenium (sneezeweed)
Knautia
Lupinus (lupin)
Lychnis (catchfly)

Lythrum (purple loosestrife)
Macleaya (plume poppy)
Mentha (mint)
Monarda (bergamot)
Nepeta (catmint)
Perovskia (Russian sage)
Phlox
Platycodon (balloon flower)
Salvia (sage)
Scabiosa (scabious, pincushion flower)
Sedum (stonecrop)
Senecio (some)
Solidago (golden rod)
Verbena
Viola

Division

The division of perennial plants is one of the easiest and most frequently used methods of propagation. It is done not only to produce new plants, but also as a means of keeping existing plants healthy and free from congestion. The basic idea behind division is that the plants involved do not have a single root, but a mass of roots emerging from all parts of the plant that touch the soil or are actually in the soil. A new plant can be formed simply by breaking a part of the plant away with some roots attached.

SUITABLE CANDIDATES
A large number of perennials can be increased through division. Most of the clump- or mat-forming plants are easy to divide. A plant can usually be divided if it consists of several "noses" or growing points. Division is another vegetative method of propagation, and each of the divisions will resemble the parent plant.

WHEN AND HOW TO DIVIDE
The best time for dividing most plants is just as they are coming into growth, usually in spring. Some, especially those with shallow, fibrous roots like asters, can be divided at any time as long as they are kept moist during dry weather, but even these are best dealt with in spring.

A suitable time is when you are busy with the spring tidy-up. Any old or congested plants can then be dug up, divided and replanted. This is, in fact, an essential part of the maintenance of many herbaceous plants, which would otherwise die out in the centre of the clump and might soon die out altogether.

Dig up the clump to be divided and work on it in the border, if it is a simple division, or in a potting shed, greenhouse, or at least on a table, if the plant is to be propagated. You will need the young growth around the outside of the clump. The centre is usually old and congested, and should be thrown away.

The simplest way of dividing the clump, especially for tougher plants like asters, is to place it on the ground and insert two forks back to back. When the forks are levered apart, the roots are pulled with it, and you will have two plants. Repeat this process until the plant is in small pieces. This is, however, a rather crude method, and the plant can be damaged, allowing in disease.

Left: *Hellebores can be increased through division.*

PERENNIALS THAT CAN BE DIVIDED

Acanthus (bear's breeches)
Achillea (yarrow)
Aconitum (monkshood; this plant is poisonous)
Adenophora (gland bellflower)
Agapanthus (African lily)
Anaphalis (pearl everlasting)
Anemone
Anthemis
Artemisia (wormwood)
Aster (Michaelmas daisy)
Astilbe
Astrantia (masterwort)
Bergenia (elephant's ears)
Campanula (bellflower; some)
Convallaria (lily-of-the-valley)
Coreopsis (tickseed)
Crambe
Delphinium
Epilobium (willowherb)
Epimedium
Euphorbia (spurge; some)
Galega (goat's rue)
Geranium (cranesbill; some)
Helenium (sneezeweed)
Helianthus (sunflower)
Helleborus (hellebore)
Hemerocallis (daylily)
Heuchera (coral bells)
Hosta
Hylomecon japonica
Inula
Iris
Kniphofia (red-hot poker)
Lamium (dead nettle)
Liatris (gay feathers)
Ligularia (leopard plant)
Lobelia
Lychnis (catchfly)
Lysimachia (yellow loosestrife)

Lythrum (purple loosestrife)
Meconopsis (blue poppy)
Mentha (mint)
Monarda (bergamot)
Nepeta (catmint)
Ophiopogon
Paeonia (peony)
Persicaria (knotweed)
Phlomis
Phormium tenax (New Zealand flax)
Physostegia (obedient plant)
Polemonium (Jacob's ladder)
Polygonatum (Solomon's seal)
Potentilla (cinquefoil)
Primula
Pulmonaria (lungwort)
Ranunculus (buttercup, crowfoot)
Ranzania
Rheum (ornamental rhubarb)
Rudbeckia (coneflower)
Salvia (sage; some)
Saponaria (soapwort)
Scabiosa (scabious, pincushion flower)
Schizostylis coccinea (Kaffir lily)
Sedum (stonecrop)
Sidalcea (prairie mallow)
Smilacina
Solidago (golden rod)
Stachys
Symphytum (comfrey)
Tanacetum
Thalictrum (meadow rue)
Tradescantia
Trollius (globeflower)
Uvularia (merrybells)
Vancouveria
Vernonia (ironweed)
Veronica (speedwell)

SIMPLE DIVISION

1 Water the plant to be divided during the previous day. Dig up a clump of the plant, in this case the Michaelmas daisy, *Aster novi-belgii*.

2 Insert two forks back-to-back into the plant and lever apart by pushing the handles together. Keep on dividing until the pieces are of the required size.

3 The pieces of the plant can be replaced in the bed, but dig over the soil first, removing any weeds and adding some well-rotted organic material.

4 Alternatively, small pieces of the plant can be potted up individually. After watering, place these in a closed cold frame for a few days, before hardening off.

DIVISION BY HAND

A better method is to divide the plant with your fingers. Hold the plant in both hands and shake it so that the earth begins to fall off. At the same time, gently pull the plant apart. Many plants – primulas and sisyrinchiums, for example – seem to fall apart in your hands.

If your soil is heavy and sticky, it will not fall off easily, or, if the plants have very tangled roots, it can be difficult to separate them. However, if you hold the plant under water and manipulate it in the same way, a surprising number of plants will come apart quite easily, without damaging the roots.

Some plants will not separate easily and will need to be cut. Wash off all the soil so that the growing points can be seen and then cut cleanly through the main root that is holding them together. This limits the damage to the plant. Cutting a plant into pieces with a spade will work, but you are likely to cut through so many roots that wounds are left through which infection can take hold.

Larger divisions can be replanted directly back in the soil as long as the weather is not too hot and dry; dull, damp weather is ideal. Firm them in and keep watered until they become established. Before replanting, it is a good idea to remove any weeds and to rejuvenate the soil by digging in some compost.

When a plant is divided into smaller pieces it is best to re-establish the plant by growing it on in a pot before planting out. This is important if you want to sell or give away the plants. Once you have made the division, pot it up into an appropriately sized pot, using a good quality potting compost (soil mix).

Label and water the pot and then place it in an enclosed environment such as a shady cold frame or greenhouse. Make sure that you do not place the pots in direct sunlight. Water and grow the plants on until they are established, when they can be hardened off and then planted out or sold.

DIVIDING BY HAND

1 Dig up a section of the plant, large enough to provide the quantity of material that you require.

2 Hold the plant firmly at the base and shake it vigorously so that the soil falls off and the roots are exposed.

3 Gently pull the plant into individual pieces, simply by manipulating it with your hands. Many plants, such as this sisyrinchium, will come apart very easily.

4 The pieces should now be potted up individually using a good compost (soil mix). Place in a shaded cold frame for a few days and then harden off.

Above: *Some geraniums can be increased through division.*

DIVIDING UNDER WATER

1 Many plants, such as these kniphofias, have very tangled roots or are growing in heavy soils that will not easily fall away.

2 Shake the plants in a bucket of water so that the soil is washed from the roots. Wash with a hosepipe if the soil is very difficult to remove.

3 Once the soil is washed away, most plants break up surprisingly easily into individual sections, each with a growing point.

4 Some plants do not come apart very easily. If this is the case, cut the sections apart with a sharp knife, making certain that each section has a bud.

5 Once the plants have been cleaned and divided, they can be potted up individually and then kept in a shaded frame until they have recovered.

Taking Root Cuttings

As anyone who has accidentally left a section of root in the ground from a dandelion or dock while weeding will know only too well, it is possible to grow some plants from a small piece of root. This is not a large group of plants, but for some, such as named pasqueflowers (*Pulsatilla*) and oriental poppies (*Papaver orientale*), it is the only satisfactory method of reproduction.

SUITABLE PLANTS

Because it is a vegetative method of propagation, the plants grown from root cuttings will be identical to the parent. The plants from which such cuttings are taken are generally those with thick, fleshy roots, especially those with taproots. Often there is no other way of propagating these plants, because division is impossible and stem cuttings do not work. Seed can often be taken, but there is no guarantee that the plants will resemble the parent.

The best time to take root cuttings is during the plant's dormant period, which normally means the winter, and because growth often starts below ground well before the end of winter, the usual time for taking such cuttings is early winter.

Usually the plant to be propagated is dug up and the roots detached, but it is possible to dig down the side of a plant and remove one or two roots, without disturbing the whole plant. This is the safest way of dealing with a precious plant. Remove a root by cutting directly across it at right angles. Then trim the lower end with a slanting cut at about 45 degrees so that it is about 5cm (2in) long. The purpose of making these two distinct cuts is to make it obvious which is the top and which is the bottom of the cutting. This is important because there may be no distinguishing marks, and it is all too easy to plant them upside down by accident.

Fill a pot with cutting compost (planting mix) and firm it down by tapping it on a bench or table. Make a vertical hole with a pencil or piece of dowel and slip the cutting into it, making certain that the horizontal cut is at the top, which should be just below the surface of the compost. Several roots can be placed in one pot.

Water and set the pot in a cold frame for the winter. With the coming of spring, shoots should appear above the compost and closer examination should reveal new roots beginning to appear on the cutting. Once you are sure that there are roots, pot them up in individual pots and treat as any new young plant.

Above: *The elegant* Acanthus spinosus *is among those perennials that can be propagated by taking root cuttings. The pale mauve and white flowers appear in summer.*

Above: *Primulas, in this case a candelabra primula, can be increased by taking root cuttings.*

TAKING ROOT CUTTINGS

1 Carefully dig the plant from the ground, ensuring that the thicker roots come out intact.

2 Wash the soil from the roots and then remove one or more of the thicker ones.

3 Cut the roots into 5–8cm (2–3in) lengths with a horizontal cut at the top and a slanting cut at the bottom.

4 Fill the pot with a cutting compost (planting mix) and insert the cuttings vertically with the horizontal cut at the top, so that they are just level with the surface.

5 Cover the compost and the top of the cuttings with a layer of fine grit. Water and place in a cold frame.

ANNUALS

Annuals are tremendously popular with gardeners. In general they are easy to grow, often thriving in poor, dry soil, and will produce a brilliant show of colour over a long period of time. There are also many delicate, subtle colours, as well as the familiar bold and bright varieties. Annuals are perfect for bedding schemes, as formal or informal as you like, or they can be allowed to self-seed, in which case many varieties will more or less take care of themselves. Then again, if you only have space for a window box or a hanging basket, you can still create a stunning display. This chapter is the perfect introduction to the range of possibilities of annuals, from advice on design to practical information enabling you to achieve your gardening goals.

Left: Cosmos comes in a wide range of pinks, reds, oranges and yellows, and flowers for a long period. This lovely dark pink one is 'Versailles Tetra'.

ANNUALS DEFINED

What is an Annual?

The definition of annuals is not quite as straightforward as it might seem at first sight. Fundamentally, annuals are plants that grow and die within one year, but in gardening terms we usually think of them as plants that we use during the course of one year only and then discard, even though they might, in certain conditions, live longer. This means that the definition also encompasses biennial plants as well as a few tender and short-lived perennials.

TRUE ANNUALS

True annuals are those that grow from seed each year, flower and then die, with only the seeds surviving to the following year. Some annuals, such as those used as bedding plants or for containers, *Lobelia* for example, have a very long season and will flower from the beginning of summer right through until the middle or end of autumn. Others, however, such as the amusingly named poached egg plant (*Limnanthes douglasii*), have a brief but dramatic flowering of perhaps only a couple of weeks or even less. In addition to length of flowering, there are also other characteristics that differentiate different types of annuals.

HARDY ANNUALS

One of the most useful types of annual, especially for use in mixed plantings, are the hardy annuals. These can be sown directly into the soil or in trays or pots to be planted out in autumn where they will survive the winter unprotected, ready to produce flowers in the late spring or early summer, well before the more tender bedding comes into flower. Forget-me-nots (*Myosotis*) are a good example of this.

HALF-HARDY ANNUALS

Half-hardy annuals will not tolerate frost and should be either grown from seed in a greenhouse or conservatory and planted out once the danger of frosts has passed or sown directly into the soil once temperatures are guaranteed to be above freezing. Those sown directly into the soil will flower much later than those that have been raised under glass in the spring and planted out as almost mature plants, and in some cases as fully mature plants in full flower. Anything grown under protection needs to be fully hardened off before it is planted outside. Examples of half-hardy annuals include French marigolds (*Tagetes patula*) and cosmos. Sometimes a distinction is made between half-hardy annuals and tender ones (see below).

TENDER ANNUALS

Tender annuals originate in tropical and sub-tropical climates and must be raised under heat in a greenhouse in order for them to flower within a year. If they were sown in the open soil after the danger of frosts had passed, they would not have a long enough season to mature and flower before the autumn frosts. The castor-oil plant (*Ricinus*) is a good example.

SOME POPULAR ANNUALS

Ageratum (floss flower)
Amaranthus caudatus (love-lies-bleeding)
Antirrhinum (snapdragon)
Calceolaria
Centaurea cyanus (cornflower)
Cosmos
Godetia
Ipomoea

Limnanthes douglasii (poached egg plant)
Myosotis (forget-me-not)
Nigella damascena (love-in-a-mist)
Papaver somniferum (opium poppy)
Petunia
Tagetes (marigold)
Tropaeolum (nasturtium)

Top: *This drift of the annual* Cleome *'Pink Queen' combines well with perennials in a mixed border. The effect of the foliage of these plants is nearly as striking as that of the flowers.*

Left: *Tender perennials are particularly good subjects for containers because they can be moved inside at the end of the season. Here a scented pelargonium, variegated fuchsia and* Persicaria captita *are displayed behind a creeping thyme.*

Right: *Brightly-coloured pelargoniums and mesembryanthemum create a spectacular display when used in this colourful bedding scheme. The scheme is unusual in that it has been created in a rock garden.*

What is a Biennial?

True annuals have a life-span of less than 12 months, and always flower within this time span. On the other hand, there are also biennials which take longer to flower. Biennials germinate in the first year, overwinter as a rosette of leaves and then flower during the following spring or summer. Occasionally biennials may be slow growing in their first year. If this is the case, the flowers may take an extra year to appear, blooming only in their third year.

TYPICAL BIENNIAL

The well-known foxglove, *Digitalis purpurea*, is a typical biennial. It is sown in the spring of the first year, either in trays or directly into the ground, and then it quickly germinates. Foxgloves grow on throughout the year with their basal leaves reaching almost full size before the start of the winter. They are fully hardy and need no winter protection. As spring of the second year approaches foxgloves grow rapidly, forming the familiar tall flower spike, which by early summer forms a statuesque spire of flowers.

SELF-SOWING

If left after flowering, foxgloves will produce copious amounts of seed which self-sow to produce another crop of plants. There are quite a number of biennials that behave in this way, which can save the gardener a lot of time. All that is required is to remove any excess or unwanted plants as well as any that have sown themselves in the wrong place.

Some plants often skip a year, the seed lying dormant then germinating the following year. *Delphinium staphisagria* and the Scotch thistle (*Onopordum acanthium*) often behave like this, but after a few years there is enough residual seed in the soil for at least some to germinate every year giving a succession of flowers every year.

DIRECT SOWING

Many biennials and some short-lived perennials that are treated as biennials, such as wallflowers (*Erysimum*) and sweet William (*Dianthus barbatus*), are sown directly into the soil. They can also be sown in trays but do better in the ground. They should be sown in shallow drills in the late spring and thinned out when they have germinated. They are left in the rows until the autumn, when they will be big enough for transferring to their final flowering positions, which will often be an area of border that has just been cleared of the current year's annuals after the flowers have faded.

SOME POPULAR BIENNIALS

Anchusa capensis (Cape forget-me-not)
Brassica oleracea (ornamental cabbage)
Campanula medium (Canterbury bells)
Delphinium staphisagria
Dianthus barbatus (sweet William)
Digitalis purpurea (foxglove)
Echium vulgare (viper's bugloss)
Eryngium giganteum (Miss Willmott's Ghost)
Erysimum, syn. *Cheiranthus* (wallflower)
Exacum affine
Glaucium flavum (horned poppy)
Hesperis matronalis (sweet rocket)
Lunaria annua (honesty)
Matthiola incana (Brompton stock)
Oenothera biennis (evening primrose)
Onopordum acanthium (Scotch thistle)
Papaver nudicaule (Iceland poppy)
Silybum marianum
Verbascum (mullein)

Left: *Biennials, such as this foxglove,* Digitalis purpurea, *usually form a rosette during their first year. After overwintering, they grow during the next spring to flower in the summer.*

Above: Eryngium giganteum, *which is also commonly known as Miss Willmott's Ghost, produces steely blue flowers and has silver, prickly foliage. It is a good flower for drying.*

Right: Lunaria annua *is, in spite of its name, a biennial. Also known as honesty, its delicate silvery seed cases are very valuable in dried flower arrangements and decorations.*

Above: Hesperis matronalis *or sweet rocket is an old-fashioned cottage garden plant that has a most delightful scent, which is especially apparent around dusk.*

What is a Tender Perennial?

Gardeners are often unaware that many of the 'annuals' they grow every year are, in fact, perennials, which in their wild state will go on flowering year after year. There are two reasons why these plants are treated as annuals in temperate regions. Some are short-lived while others are tender and would not survive a frosty winter. With care, both types could be treated as perennials, but their natures are such that it is advisable to discard the plants at the end of the year and then start afresh the following year.

SHORT-LIVED PERENNIALS

These can be typified by wallflowers (*Erysimum*), snapdragons (*Antirrhinum*) and sweet Williams (*Dianthus barbatus*). Traditionally, these are sown afresh each year for flowering the next. However, if they are grown in soil that does not become too water-logged, and are trimmed back after flowering, they will flower again the following year, and even the next. However, with each year the flowering becomes a little less successful and to get the best show it is best to treat them as an annual or biennial and sow each year.

Being perennial they can also be propagated vegetatively. If the sown seed produces a wallflower that has an interesting colouring, it is possible to ensure that you have it again the next year by taking cuttings from non-flowering stems. Treat these as ordinary cuttings, potting them up when they have rooted and planting out in the autumn for flowering the following year.

TENDER PERENNIALS

Different types of tender perennials are treated in various ways by gardeners. Some, including petunias, are grown exactly like annuals, which means that they are sown every year and discarded after flowering. Another group, which includes pelargoniums and fuchsias, can be propagated by cuttings in the autumn, overwintered in a greenhouse or on a windowsill, and then planted out the following spring after the danger of frosts has passed. A third group includes dahlias and tuberous begonias, and these have tubers which are simply lifted, stored in a frost-free place over the winter, and then planted out again.

SOME POPULAR TENDER PERENNIALS

Abutilon
Alonsoa warscewiczii (mask flower)
Alternanthera
Antirrhinum majus (snapdragon)
Argyranthemum
Begonia semperflorens
Bellis perennis (daisy)
Browallia speciosa
Capsicum annuum (ornamental pepper)
Celosia cristata
Chrysanthemum
Cobaea scandens (cup and saucer vine)
Coleus blumei (syn. *Solenostemon scutellarioides*)
Commelina coelestris
Coreopsis (tickseed)
Crepis rubra
Cuphea miniata
Dahlia
Eccremocarpus scandens (Chilean glory flower)
Erysimum (syn. *Cheiranthus*) *cheiri* (wallflower)
Erysimum hieraciifolium
Felicia amelloides (blue marguerite)
Gaillardia aristata (blanket flower)
Gazania
Gomphrena globosa

Helichrysum
Heliotropium arborescens (syn. *H. peruvianum*)
Hesperis matronalis (sweet rocket)
Humea elegans
Impatiens (busy Lizzie)
Limonium sinuatum
Melianthus major (honeybush)
Mimulus
Mirabilis jalapa (marvel of Peru)
Nicotiana langsdorfii
Nierembergia rivularis
Osteospermum
Pelargonium (geranium)
Polygonum capitatum (syn. *Persicaria capitata*)
Primula
Ricinus communis (castor-oil plant)
Rudbeckia hirta (coneflower)
Salvia farinacea
Senecio cineraria (syn. *S. maritima*)
Solanum pseudocapsicum (Jerusalem cherry)
Tanacetum ptarmicaeflorum
Thunbergia alata (black-eyed Susan)
Verbena × hybrida
Viola × wittrockiana (pansy)

Above: *Several salvias, including this* Salvia farinacea, *are popular 'annuals', but they are, in fact, perennials and can be overwintered in warmer areas.*

Left: *Dahlias are an ideal choice for bringing the summer to a colourful end. However, dahlias are frost tender and must be lifted and stored in a frost-free place, such as a greenhouse or conservatory, before the weather turns cold. This striking, rich orange variety is 'David Howard'.*

Right: Begonia semperflorens *will flower non-stop from early summer through to the end of autumn when it will be killed by the first frosts if it is not moved inside.*

Choosing a Scheme

Although large bedding schemes are not as popular as they once were, there is a revival of interest in the various ways that annual plants can be used and they are being appreciated anew. One of the main advantages of using annuals is their great versatility: they can be mixed with other plants or they can be used on their own.

ANNUAL VARIETY

The great thing about annuals is that they only last for one year. This may seem rather a waste, but the advantage is that once they have been planted you are not tied to a particular scheme for more than a year. If you so wish you can repeat it again the following year, but, on the other hand, you can do something completely different every year. You can simply vary the way you use the plants, that is by choosing another pattern or colour scheme, or you can use quite different plants.

THINKING AHEAD

While annuals provide summer and early autumn enjoyment in the garden, they can also be a source of much pleasure during the winter months as you plan your planting schemes for the following year. While this may simply appear to be a pleasant way of spending a winter's evening, such advance planning is very important, especially if you wish to use annuals on any scale. You need to have worked out well in advance exactly what you want to do and what you will need to achieve it. There is nothing more annoying than

devising a scheme only to discover that when you come to lay it out several plant varieties or colours are missing or you cannot get hold of them.

You can always obtain a few plants from the local garden centre or nursery, but buying in any quantity can become expensive, and you may be restricted in your choice. A much better plan, if you have time and space, is to grow your own plants. This way you can grow as many as you need (plus a few spares), and to your own satisfaction, rather than being limited to what may be second-rate plants from some other source.

INSPIRATION

Some people can invent their own schemes but many others need to look for inspiration elsewhere. Look at gardening books and magazines and visit as many gardens as you can.

Above: *This arrangement is simplicity itself. Scarlet pelargoniums with decorative leaves can be used to provide a very sophisticated display simply by growing them in terracotta pots and lining them up on top of a wall. You can, of course, use as many pots as you want.*

Right: *Busy Lizzies* (Impatiens) *create a colourful bed that contrasts well with the surrounding green hedge. Planting in blocks of the same colour rather than mixing colours is more restful to the eye.*

Above: *Annuals can be planted to create striking points of interest, as this casual display of evening primroses* (Oenothera biennis) *shows.*

Right: *Annuals are excellent plants for edging borders. Here, French marigolds* (Tagetes patula) *line a small patio bed.*

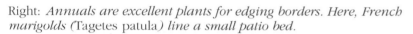

Above: *Annuals have been used here to create a large bedding scheme of subtle colouring. These bedding schemes are very effective but need a lot of careful planning.*

Informal Schemes

One of the most common ways of using bedding plants is to plant them in an informal way. Whether roughly grouped or arranged in some form of pattern, they are basically planted in a glorious mixture that is rather reminiscent of old cottage gardens. While the longer-lasting bedding plants can produce a lovely display, and are invaluable for those with limited time, you can create much more interesting effects by using some of the more unusual annuals with relatively short flowering periods, thus changing the picture as the season progresses.

DESIGN WITH CARE

Mixing plants without any real thought to their placement may well produce a riot of colour, but it can equally produce a chaotic mess. Most gardeners have probably come across examples of front gardens covered in a garish mixture of red, white, blue and orange all stirred up leaving an uncomfortable spectacle on which there is no place for the eye to rest. Take care when mixing the colours in beds and borders and try not to make the effect look too random and unplanned. Make the colours blend, the soft colours creating a restful scene, the brighter ones livening up the overall picture.

SEASONAL ANNUALS

In an informal setting, rather than the more typical bedding plants, less garish plants can often be used to create a bed that has more lasting interest. In spring, the soft colours of forget-me-nots (*Myosotis*), with foxgloves (*Digitalis*) pushing up through them and starting to flower before the forget-me-nots are over, are delightful. These can be followed by nigellas growing around the foxgloves which in turn can be replaced by stately mulleins (*Verbascum*). Later in the season both the yellow Mexican poppy (*Argemone mexicana*) and the white (*A. grandiflora*) might add their own charm. *Crepis rubra*, a short-lived perennial, and *Silene pendula* can be used to add a soft pink note to the planting. Pale cream could also perhaps be introduced by planting *Collomia grandiflora*.

All these mixed colours will vary from week to week, creating a constantly changing, soft misty background against which splashes of eye-catching colour, perhaps the bright red of field poppies (*Papaver rhoeas*), can be added to liven it up.

Top right: *Cottage-garden simplicity and informality has been created by weaving* Collomia grandiflora *through perennials and other annuals.*

Right: *A closer shot of the above showing the way informal plantings can be random without looking too 'bitty'.*

Right: *A mixture of annuals and perennials draws the eye along a path to the front door. Here, the informality creates a wonderfully welcoming atmosphere. This contrasts well with the more formal outlines of the house. Remember that this type of gardening is not restricted to quaint cottages.*

Below: *A mass of different annuals creates the effect of a colourful meadow. Such plantings are not easy to achieve but are well worth the effort.*

Below right: *This is a semi-formal scheme in which the annuals have been beautifully planted in blocks but not to any overall pattern.*

Formal Patterns

Patterns have always played an important part in garden design, especially in the larger gardens where there was space to lay things out on a grand scale. The grand designs are now seen only in municipal plantings, especially on the coast and in parks and other public spaces. For many years they have languished, but now a new generation of gardeners has produced a revival with some very imaginative plantings. There is no reason why the gardener with only a small plot should not produce scaled-down versions of these.

STRAIGHT LINES AND SQUIGGLES

All types of patterns can be used as long as they are not so intricate that the detail is lost as the plants grow. The plot to be planted can be divided up into geometrical shapes, such as straight lines, squares, rectangles, triangles, circles and so on. An alternative is to use free-form lines and shapes that interlock or at least react with one another to produce a pleasing pattern. Scrolls and teardrops might be two examples. Each of the lines or shapes can be delineated or filled in with a different colour of flower or leaf. It is worth remembering that foliage adds a great deal to these schemes.

PICTURES

For those who want to do something special, creating a picture with flowers and foliage can be quite a challenge, and can be stunning when carried out well. At a municipal park level, one often sees the town's coat of arms (emblem) picked out in plants. Another popular theme is to make a working clock from flowers and foliage, with only the hands being made of metal or plastic. These types of designs are not only complicated and challenging but need a great deal of attention, especially with clipping, to keep them from going ragged and losing their image.

FROM PAPER TO THE BED

Patterns, especially intricate ones, need a great deal of planning and thought. They should be worked out on graph paper in the same way that you might work out an embroidery or tapestry. You should then stretch a grid, using string and canes, across the plot to be planted, corresponding to the grid on the drawing. Using the string grid as a guide to position, you can then transfer the design to the ground by outlining the shapes with sand poured from a bottle.

Right: *Although the planting in this urn is informal, the overall effect, especially with the begonias around the base, is formal, without being too rigid.*

Left: *Annuals arranged in simple geometric shapes create a satisfying rhythm along this long border. Blocks of single colours are easier on the eye than random mixes.*

Right: *With plenty of space to play with, creating a scheme like this is very gratifying. However, with a little ingenuity and good planning, there is no reason why such a scheme cannot be incorporated into a much smaller garden.*

Above: *A simple scheme using bold colours.*

Above: *A rainbow of colours can look wonderfully cheerful.*

Carpet Schemes

A long-standing tradition in public parks and gardens, carpet schemes can be used in a variety of ways. You can create intricate, formal designs, as demonstrated here, or you can use blocks of colour in bold, simple shapes, or a more informal, irregular scheme. The blocks can be created by planting out bedding plants, or you can sow directly into the soil, broadcasting different seed over each area. Striking colour contrasts can be achieved with flowers, or an interesting effect can be produced using only foliage plants. Many gardeners are under the impression that they do not have enough space for a carpet scheme, but if only small, low-growing plants are used, a very impressive design can be created in a relatively small area.

PURE BLOCKS

Carpet bedding can be arranged in some form of pattern, possibly using an edging plant in a contrasting or sympathetic colour. The blocks can be regular in shape for a formal effect or they can be more random in appearance, perhaps with their edges in a series of curves if you want to achieve a more informal look.

The edges of a block are usually clear-cut, one type of plant ends and another starts, but there is no reason why they should not merge, especially if the colours blend well. The blocks can consist purely of one colour, bright red salvias for example, or they can be a subtle or contrasting mixture. Soft blue forget-me-nots (*Myosotis*) and pink tulips may be an unoriginal combination but it is nonetheless a very effective one. If you need inspiration for devising carpet bedding schemes, look at your local park or public gardens where they are common.

WORKING IN THREE DIMENSIONS

It is worth remembering at the planning stage that different plants grow to different heights and spread, so make allowances for this. Otherwise the design may look ragged. On the other hand, it may be possible to use the different heights to advantage to create a three-dimensional bed with some areas, or even certain plants, higher than others.

PLANNING

It can be fun to work out different designs for carpet bedding schemes. For a formal scheme, you will need to draw the design on graph paper and mark out the grid on the ground using canes and string. Then draw the outline of the design on the ground by pouring sand from a bottle. If you want a less formal scheme, the sizes and shapes of the blocks of colour will be less critical and you can draw the design freehand on the ground with sand.

PLANTING A CARPET BEDDING SCHEME

1 Plan the scheme and draw it on graph paper. To transfer the design to the ground, first mark out a grid using canes and string, then draw out the design using distinctively coloured sand or compost (soil mix), poured from a container. If you are using plants to mark out the design, plant these first, along the lines of sand or compost (soil mix). Complete the planting by filling in between the lines with plants, following your plan. To avoid treading on the plants as you work, use a platform. Here, ladders supported on bricks, with timber planks placed along the rungs, have been used.

2 The finished scheme illustrates the benefit of patient work. Maintenance can be carried out using the same bridging technique as was used for its construction. Maintenance consists of removing any weeds and cutting back any growth that gets too long.

Left: *A wonderfully ornate bed using many of the same plants as the detailed scheme (see below). This type of scheme can be carried out on a grand scale if space allows or devised to fit a small front garden. Much fun can be had during the winter, devising the scheme and drawing up the plans.*

Left: *The plants used in this scheme are (from the left): rows 1-3 forms of* Alternanthera*; 4* Sempervivum arachnoideum*; 5* Tanacetum parthenium *'Golden Moss'; 6* Senecio serpens*; 7* Alternanthera*; 8* Sedum spathulifolium *'Cape Blanco'; 9* Echeveria glauca*; 10* Sedum spathulifolium *'Purpureum'; 11* Echeveria secunda*.*

Parterres

Gardeners with space to spare can create a superior bedding scheme by planting a parterre and filling it with annuals. Parterres are patterns, either geometric or free-flowing, where each element is outlined by a low hedge. Where there is enough space, patterns can become very intricate and are often best viewed from above, perhaps from the top floor of the house. However, it is possible to create a small parterre in a relatively small garden. Indeed the simplicity of such a garden and the relatively low maintenance it requires lends itself to this type of situation.

HEDGES

The only real disadvantage of this type of scheme is that you have to wait several years for the hedges to grow to the required dimensions. The best plant to use is undoubtedly box (*Buxus sempervirens*), which is, unfortunately, very slow growing. This is an advantage in that it only needs cutting once or perhaps twice a year, but it does take some years to mature. A more rapid design can be achieved by using *Teucrium chamaedrys* or the grey-leaved *Santolina pinnata neapolitana*, but both need trimming a little more frequently than box. Lavender (*Lavandula*) is more untidy but makes a very colourful and fragrant parterre.

The hedges should be about 25cm (10in) high. Prepare the ground well and be certain to remove any perennial weeds or these will cause a problem later on. Dig in plenty of organic material as the hedge is likely to be there for many years and the better the condition of the soil, the better the condition of the hedge, especially if drought conditions prevail.

THE INFILL

Make the most of the parterre and fill it with winter bedding plants as well as using it to create a colourful summer effect. Pansies are ideal for winter use. For spring, use forget-me-nots, primulas and wallflowers (*Erysimum*) as well as bulbs like tulips and narcissus.

For summer the choice is enormous. Each section of the parterre can show a different colour, or colours can be mixed. Traditional bedding plants that have a regularity in height and spread, a long flowering period and require little attention also make ideal candidates. Remember that foliage plants are excellent fillers – colourful *Coleus* (syn. *Solenostemon*), for example, or the subtle *Helichrysum petiolare*.

PERMANENCE

Since the hedges take a while to grow, the basic shapes in the parterre cannot be changed each year. This makes annuals an ideal choice for filling the beds – they will not only vary from season to season but can be completely changed from year to year.

Above: *The edges of the parterre in this walled garden are made up of box (*Buxus sempervirens*) and filled with striking Salvia farinacea 'Victoria'.*

ANNUALS FOR FILLING A PARTERRE

Begonia semperflorens
Bellis (daisy)
Coleus blumei (syn.
  Solenostemon
  scutellarioides)
Erysimum, syn. *Cheiranthus*,
  cheiri (wallflower)
Helichrysum petiolare

Heliotropium
Impatiens (busy Lizzie)
Lobelia erinus
Myosotis (forget-me-not)
Pelargonium (geranium)
Primula
Salvia patens
Tagetes (marigold)

Above: *Wallflowers* (Erysimum*) are superb plants for creating mass planting within a parterre. The variation in their colour establishes an overall effect, rather than the uneven one that mixing colours can often create.*

Left: *Complicated patterns, like this one with its sinuous curves, call for a simple planting, here fulfilled by using yellow pansies (*Viola × wittrockiana*).*

Mixed Borders

Annual plants do not have to be used exclusively on their own in borders or beds devoted to various types of bedding scheme. They can be mixed with other plants, perennials and shrubs. This has the advantage of vastly increasing the variety of plants that can be used in the border (enlarging the gardener's palette, in other words), as well as allowing the introduction of a variable element into what is otherwise a fixed planting. A perennial border will vary slightly from year to year as the influence of the seasons and weather alters timing and the amount of flowering, but generally this type of border will remain much the same in appearance. By using different annuals, perhaps introducing reds instead of blues, or yellows instead of white, the overall effect can be subtly altered.

CHOOSING PLANTS

Many of the popular bedding plants, such as red pelargoniums, are too rigid for the mixed border. It is better if possible to use annuals that look at home among herbaceous plants in a perennial or mixed border. Foxgloves (*Digitalis*) are ideal for early summer, and the opium poppy (*Papaver somniferum*) for later in the season. Both work well in a cottage-garden border. A more modern border with subtle colourings might include purple-leaved red orach (*Atriplex hortensis* 'Rubra') or soft blue love- in-a-mist (*Nigella damascena*). Foliage plants like *Helichrysum petiolare* add colour or act as linking themes between colours.

PERENNIAL ANNUALS

Some annuals self-sow regularly, reappearing every year without the gardener having to bother about sowing or planting them.

These work well in a mixed border where the seed can germinate and seedlings develop undisturbed, unlike in bedding areas where the soil is dug over every year, and self-sowing plants can be a nuisance. Many self-seeding plants, such as borage (*Borago officinalis*), also associate well with a herbaceous border.

PLANTING

If the annual plants are to be dotted about the border, as foxgloves might be, they can be planted directly in their positions. For a drift, however, or even a block of plants, it is preferable to dig over the area first and rejuvenate the soil with well rotted organic material. When planting, avoid setting out the plants in straight rows. An uneven number of plants makes this easier, three or five making a more satisfactory arrangement than, say, two or four. Remove the plants after flowering.

1 Remove any old plants and weeds from the area. Dig over the soil, avoiding disturbing the roots of nearby plants, and add well-rotted organic material if the soil has not been rejuvenated recently. If necessary, only dig the centre of the patch, where the plants will actually be positioned; their foliage will spread to fill the gap.

2 Feed the soil by scattering a slow-release general fertilizer, following the manufacturer's instructions.

3 Work the fertilizer into the soil using a rake. If you are going to sow seed, break the soil down to a fine tilth at the same time. For bedding plants, the soil need not be as fine – an attractive, even tilth is sufficient.

5 If you wish to use bedding plants to fill the gap, simply plant them out at the appropriate intervals to the same depths they were in their pots. Gently firm in each plant, then rake the soil to even it and to remove any footprints. Water thoroughly.

4 If you want to sow a drift of annuals, scatter the seed evenly over the ground. Rake in and water using a watering can fitted with a fine rose. If the ground is very dry, water and allow the water to drain away before sowing, then sow and water again. When the seedlings appear, thin them to the desired distance apart.

Above: *In this beautifully informal border, the annuals that have been chosen blend in perfectly with the perennials. Formal bedding plants would look completely out of place in such a planting scheme.*

Temporary Fillers

The fact that annuals only last for a year can be put to good use, not only by giving the gardener scope to vary the display from year to year but also by providing an ideal material for a temporary filler. There are two principal ways in which they can be used for this purpose: firstly to fill a whole bed for a year or two, and secondly to occupy space while the principal plants in the border are filling out.

LYING FALLOW

There are often good reasons for not planting a new permanent border in haste. It makes sense to fill in any temporary spaces between the shrubs that you have planted with annuals. Ground that has not been used for some years, for example, might harbour weed seed, both annual and perennial, and if perennials are planted any resulting weeds might be difficult to remove. By planting first with annuals, which are cleared at least once a year, the border can be easily dug over and cleaned until the weed problem has diminished.

Another good reason for taking your time when designing and planting a permanent border is that you can observe it through the seasons. You will then get firmer ideas about the types of plants you would like to plant. Rushing into buying and planting a selection of shrubs could result in having to move plants around later. This is not only a waste of your energy but you also run the risk of losing expensive ones. By adding permanent plants gradually, you can see how they look in combination, and annuals are ideal for filling the gaps until the planting is complete.

FILLING THE GAPS

After planting, herbaceous plants and shrubs may take several years to reach their ultimate size. This is particularly true of shrubs. One solution is to set the plants close together and then dig up and discard some later, but this is an expensive waste and also planting too close may cause plants to malform, for example shrubs may lose their lower branches. A far better idea is to fill in the gaps with annuals. As the main plants grow the amount of space taken up by the annuals is lessened each year until they are no longer required. This keeps the ground covered, providing less opportunity for weeds to grow and creating the impression that the border is more mature than it really is. Low annuals are unlikely to harm adjacent shrubs or perennials, allowing them to develop naturally.

PLANTING

Prepare the ground well each year before planting, removing any weeds and digging in well-rotted organic matter. Make certain that the annuals are sympathetic to the main planting: without careful selection, traditional bedding plants may look out of place.

PLANTING A SHRUB BORDER

1 When first planted a shrub border will appear almost empty as it will take some years before they grow to fill the complete border. The gaps can temporarily be filled in with annuals, using fewer and fewer each year until eventually none are required as the shrubs will have taken over completely.

2 Place the pots of plants on the area to be planted to gauge the best planting distances so that all the ground will be covered. Move them around as necessary to get the best planting effect.

3 When you are satisfied with their positions, plant each one. Dig a wide hole for each plant and set the plants so that the top of the compost (soil mix) on the root ball is level with the top of the soil. Fill around the plant with soil, firm in and then water well.

5 The plants will soon settle in and spread out to cover all the space between the shrubs. This will not only be decorative, but also act as a ground-cover, helping to keep the weeds down.

4 Tidy up around the plants, levelling the surface and removing footprints. Apply a mulch around the plants if you have enough material available.

Above: Brachycome iberidifolia, *the Swan River daisy, has been used here to fill the bare ground between shrubs. Eventually the shrubs will cover all of this space.*

Annuals as Edging Plants

Many annuals make perfect plants for edging features such as paths, borders or special beds. Paths in particular benefit from an edging. A straight path with edging on either side quickly draws the eye down along its length, and will often appear longer than it really is. Edging plants also act as a visual barrier between path and border, making the scene much neater as the bustle of the border stops at the line of edging plants. They can also be a physical barrier: if larger edging plants are used they actually stop the inner plants flopping over the path.

PLANTS TO USE

Any annuals can be used as edging plants but some look better than others in this defining role. Some, such as white alyssum, make compact plants that, when lined up along the edge of a bed or border, can be used almost like a narrow ribbon. These are best used where the other border plants gradually build up in height behind them. If tall plants are used immediately behind alyssum, then the latter is often swamped and the line is lost under a tangle of stems and foliage.

Other plants, such as bright red salvias, can be used to create a positive coloured line; it is impossible not to notice such a bright streak of colour.

Both alyssum and salvia make a very formal edge, but a plant with a looser nature, such as forget-me-not (*Myosotis*), will make a softer, much more diffuse edge to the border. It will merge gently with the plants ranged behind it so that it does not form an obvious line but rather a pretty ruffle along the edge of the border.

BLENDING

Edging is usually thought of as only one plant deep, but there is no reason why the line should not be thicker – two or even three plants deep. Avoid setting plants too far apart or the edge will look uneven. It is better to plant them fairly closely so that they blend together. This might be difficult to achieve with compact or upright plants, so choose your plants with care.

MAKING THE LINE

Planting edging is not difficult, but it is important to get the line straight or running parallel with the edge of the border or path as any deviation will show up clearly. Use a garden line or some other guide to ensure your row follows the correct line and use a measure of some sort to make certain that the plants are evenly spaced.

Right: *In this planting along the edge of a lawn, no attempt has been made to create a distinct line. Instead, poached egg plants (*Limnanthes douglasii*) create a mass of colour along the edge of the border.*

1 Prepare the soil thoroughly, removing any weeds and adding some well-rotted compost or soil conditioner if the soil is tired. Break the soil down to a fairly fine tilth. Set up a garden line at an even distance from the actual edge of the border. Using a standard measure, such as a length of stick, between the edge and each plant will ensure the line is even.

2 Plant the edging plants along the line at regular intervals, regulating the distance between each one with a measuring stick. Firm in each plant, rake over the soil and water. For an informal planting, you can insert a few plants behind the main row so that the edging merges into the other plants in the border.

Above: *An informal edging of* Chrysanthemum tenuiloba *'Golden Fleck' sprawls out over a path.*

Right: *Different shades of busy Lizzie (*Impatiens*) are beautifully set off by silver-leaved plants in an elaborate, formal edging.*

Above: *China pinks (*Dianthus chinensis*) make a pretty contribution to the edge of a bed or border as this vibrantly coloured variety shows.*

ANNUALS SUITABLE FOR EDGING

Ageratum (floss flower)	*Lobularia maritima*, syn.
Begonia semperflorens	*Alyssum maritimum*
Clarkia	(sweet alyssum)
Crepis rubra	*Myosotis* (forget-me-not)
Dianthus chinensis (China	*Primula*
pink)	*Silene pendula*
Iberis amara	*Tagetes* (marigold)
Lobelia	*Viola × wittrockiana* (pansy)

Annual Climbers

We tend to think of annuals largely as temporary additions to the structure of the garden, since they only last for one year. However, there are many climbing varieties, which, although they will not continue from year to year, can put on a surprising amount of growth in one year and contribute significantly to the overall design of the garden. For example, you can add extra height and interest to a low-level border by growing annual climbers up a series of tripods (teepees).

SUPPORTS

Annual climbers can be grown up a permanent support, such as wooden trellising on a wall or in a container, or wires fixed to a wall. Alternatively, the support can be temporary, removed annually with the remains of the plant at the end of the season. Pea-sticks make excellent temporary supports, but canes or wicker pyramids are also useful.

A charming idea is to grow the annual up through a shrub. This works particularly well with shrubs that flower in the spring and perhaps look dull for the rest of the year. Once the annual starts to bloom, it will brighten up the foliage until it stops flowering. For example, grow the yellow-flowered canary creeper (*Tropaeolum peregrinum*) up through a *Spiraea* 'Arguta'.

Climbing plants can also trail, so there is no reason why many of them cannot be planted in hanging baskets and allowed to tumble down.

CULTIVATION

Climbing plants are best when they can be grown without interruption. If their growth is checked, especially by being left in the original container for too long, they will rarely grow away well. They will become weak, with yellowing leaves. Keep potting the plants on and plant them out as soon as the weather allows. Water and feed them and they will respond with vigorous growth and plenty of flowers.

Deadheading will also help the plant to produce a continuous stream of flowers. Many plants, sweet peas (*Lathyrus odoratus*) being a good example, produce shorter flowering stems as the season progresses. This is quite normal so do not think something has gone wrong.

TEMPORARY BOUNDARIES

If you are experimenting with the layout of your garden, or perhaps wish to screen off an area such as the vegetable patch, climbing annuals can make an excellent temporary boundary. A row of sweet peas, for example, can be grown up canes to create a fragrant screen, which can easily be removed at the end of the season.

Right: Ipomoea lobata *(syn.* Mina lobata*), which is also known as the cardinal climber, climbs up a metal tripod. Such plants add height to an annual border.*

ANNUAL CLIMBERS

Asarina erubescens
Caiophora
Cobaea scandens (cup and saucer vine)
Convolvulus tricolor
Eccremocarpus scaber (Chilean glory flower)
Ipomoea
Lablab purpureus, syn. *Dolichos lablab*
Lathyrus odoratus (sweet pea)
Lathyrus sativus
Mikania scandens
Rhodochiton atrosanguineum
Thunbergia alata (black-eyed Susan)
Tropaeolum majus (Indian cress)
Tropaeolum peregrinum, syn. *T. canariense* (canary creeper)

Left: *Peas and beans that usually grow in the vegetable garden can be grown as decorative as well as productive plants. There are also a number of unusual varieties with different-coloured flowers and pods that are even more attractive.*

Below: Ipomoea lobata, *also known as* Mina lobata *and* Quamoclit lobata, *has masses of scarlet flowers that gradually change to orange, then fade to yellow and eventually white. When happy it will climb to 5m (16ft).*

Above: *In spite of being related to* Ipomoea lobata *(right)*, I. indica *has flowers that look quite different. This is one of the morning glories, known as the blue dawn flower. It is a tender perennial and can climb up to 6m (20ft).*

Self-sowing Annuals

One of the criticisms of annuals is that they are labour intensive, because they have to be raised from seed or cuttings each year, often cosseted in heat, hardened off and then planted out. However, all this is unnecessary for self-sowing annuals, which can also be called naturalizing annuals although the term often implies that they are growing in a wild situation rather than in a border.

WORKING WITH SELF-SOWERS

Self-sowing annuals involve little work and can simply be admired. Of course, unless you inherited the annuals when you first took over the garden, you also have to sow or plant them out first. But once they have flowered for the first time, they will produce seed that drops to the ground and germinates without any interference to produce another crop of flowers next year.

You may need to thin out the seedlings if they are too thick, which is often the case as many self-sowing annuals produce copious amounts of seed. Fortunately, most annual self-sowers have heavy seed which drops around the original plants and does not colonize the whole garden. Some, however, such as busy Lizzies (*Impatiens*) and poppies (*Papaver*), use an explosive mechanism, flinging the seed far and wide. To control the level of self-sowing, pull up some plants before they seed.

Once they have finished seeding, the plants have to be removed to the compost heap. Be warned, though, any seed remaining with the plants may survive the composting process, if it does not become hot enough, and go on to colonize areas over which it is spread. Forget-me-nots (*Myosotis*) are notorious for this.

TIDYING UP

Do not be in too much of a hurry to clear up the plants once the flowers have gone over; remember to leave them long enough for the seed to set and drop. In most cases this happens even before the last flowers have appeared, but in some, *Hesperis matronalis* for example, it can take a long time after the end of flowering. In this case, if you want to tidy up, remove most of the old plants but leave a few to produce enough seed. If you want to dig over an area or renovate it and feel that you might disturb the cycle of self-sowing and germination, collect a few seeds and sow them yourself, setting the whole process in motion once more.

USING SELF-SOWERS

Surprisingly, perhaps, most of the self-sowers are very good garden plants and are well worth growing. Every garden should include at least a few of these wonderful plants. As self-perpetuating annuals they are really only suitable for the border, but as plants they can of course be used in containers, window boxes and hanging baskets. Either dig up a few plants from the border (there are usually more than enough) or sow them from seed in the usual way.

1 Most self-sowing annuals will drop their seed without need for assistance. But to ensure that seed does fall on to the soil, tap ripe seed heads to dislodge and scatter the seed before discarding the dead flowers.

2 As well as scattering the seed directly on to the ground, some can be collected by tapping the seed-head over a sheet of paper. Remove any bits of seed case or other detritus and pour the seed into a paper bag, labelled with the plant's name, until it is required. Store in a cool dry place.

THINNING SELF-SOWN ANNUALS

1 Some annuals produce copious amounts of seed that result in far too many seedlings. Overcrowding leads to drawn and starved plants, so thin out the seedlings to ensure a healthy display of full-sized flowers.

3 Once you have removed all the excess plants, water the remaining ones to wash the soil down around any loosened or disturbed roots. A mulch of composted or chipped bark will help to keep the area weed-free.

2 To remove the excess seedlings, pull them out without disturbing the roots of those plants you want to keep. If you want to transplant the seedlings elsewhere, remove them carefully using a trowel or hand fork.

SELF-SOWING ANNUALS

Adlumia fungosa (Allegheny vine)
Agrostemma (corn cockle)
Alcea rosea (hollyhock)
Angelica archangelica
Antirrhinum majus (snapdragon)
Argemone mexicana (Mexican poppy)
Atriplex hortensis 'Rubra' (red orach)
Borago officinalis (borage)
Calendula officinalis (pot marigold)
Centaurea cyanus (cornflower)
Chrysanthemum segetum
Clarkia amoena
Cosmos
Digitalis purpurea (foxglove)
Eryngium giganteum (Miss Willmott's Ghost)
Eschscholzia californica

Euphorbia lathyris
Galactites tomentosa
Hesperis matronalis (sweet rocket)
Isatis tinctoria (woad)
Limnanthes douglasii (poached egg plant)
Linaria maroccana (toadflax)
Lobularia maritima, syn. *Alyssum maritimum* (sweet alyssum)
Lunaria annua (honesty)
Myosotis (forget-me-not)
Nigella
Oenothera biennis (evening primrose)
Omphalodes linifolia
Onopordum acanthium (Scotch thistle)
Papaver somniferum (opium poppy)
Silene armeria (catchfly)
Tanacetum parthenium

Annuals for Fragrance

When choosing plants for a particular design or position there are several criteria to consider. The primary ones are flower colour, good foliage and how long the plant lasts, but fragrance, which is often overlooked, is also important. Scented flowers or foliage are an added bonus in a plant and should put it at the top of your lists.

USING FRAGRANT ANNUALS

Fragrant annuals should be grown where their scent will be appreciated most. Grow some as part of a normal border so that their perfume is enjoyed when you walk past. Grow some on the patio or next to an arbour where you sit, perhaps even eat, where the relaxing atmosphere will be enhanced by the smell of fragrant flowers. These annuals can be grown in the soil or in a container. Containers are also useful for growing annuals near to windows or doors so that the perfume will waft indoors when they are open.

Heavily scented sweet peas (*Lathyrus odoratus*) are grown by many gardeners purely for cutting for the house or for giving away as fragrant posies.

TIMING

Not all fragrant annuals are perfumed all the time. The evening primrose (*Oenothera biennis*), as its name suggests, is only fragrant during the evening. The tobacco plants, *Nicotiana alata* and *N. sylvestris* in particular, are also perfumed at this time of the day. Many annuals, as with many other types of plant, will only release their odour when the weather is warm as this is when the pollinating insects that they are trying to attract will be flying. It is not worth their while to waste energy when it is too cold.

Above: *Sweet William (*Dianthus barbatus*) are related to pinks and carnations and have their own very distinctive fragrance.*

SCENTED ANNUALS

Abronia umbellatum
Brachycome iberidifolia (Swan River daisy)
Centaurea (syn. *Amberboa*) *moschata* (sweet sultan)
Datura (syn. *Brugmansia*)
Dianthus barbatus (sweet William)
Dianthus chinensis (China pink)
Erysimum, syn. *Cheiranthus* (wallflower)
Exacum affine
Heliotropium arborescens (syn. *H. peruvianum*)

Hesperis matronalis (sweet rocket)
Lathyrus odoratus (sweet pea)
Lobularia maritima, syn. *Alyssum maritimum* (sweet alyssum)
Matthiola (stock)
Mirabilis jalapa (marvel of Peru)
Nicotiana (tobacco plant)
Oenothera (evening primrose)
Pelargonium (foliage of scented-leaved only)
Phacelia
Reseda odorata (mignonette)

Above: *It is the foliage of many pelargoniums that are scented rather than the flowers. These pelargonium cuttings will provide a beautifully scented display. When lightly crushed they emit an aromatic scent.*

Above: *Sweet peas* (Lathyrus odoratus), *one of the best-loved of all fragrant annuals, can be used as trailing plants, as here, instead of their more usual climbing habit.*

Left: *Placing scented annuals near open windows can fill the room with their fragrance. Here, the delicate scent of tobacco plants* (Nicotiana) *and heliotrope* (Heliotropium) *will waft into the house.*

Above: *The tobacco plants* (Nicotiana) *release their rich scent into the evening air and are excellent plants to use near where you sit and relax at that time of day. This one is* Nicotiana langsdorfii.

Annuals for Cutting

There is no gift more welcome when visiting than a bunch of flowers from your own garden and annuals can be ideal for making up into bouquets as well as for cutting for the house. Although not all annuals are suitable for formal arrangements, nearly all of them can be made up into bunches of one sort or another. Many of the shorter ones are useful for making little posies, and even if the flower quickly wilts, the leaves may well add something to the arrangement. Some flowers, such as sweet peas, dahlias and chrysanthemums, are grown almost exclusively to use as cut flowers, while others are used both as decoration in the borders and as the occasional cutting for the house.

Above: *Because of its pendulous habit, love-lies-bleeding* (Amaranthus caudatus) *does not strike one straight away as a plant for cutting but that very quality can make it a useful choice for flower arrangements.*

WHERE TO GROW CUT FLOWERS

It is better to allocate a special piece of ground for those flowers that are grown almost exclusively for cutting, rather than try to incorporate them into a border. The problem with growing them in a border is that every time the flowers are cut, which may be regularly, it can leave a gap. Also, the constant need for access to the plants can lead to the soil becoming compacted. Growing them in a separate plot, perhaps as part of the vegetable garden, allows much easier access for cutting as well as for tending the plants.

IN THE BORDER

While it may not be a good idea to include plants that are grown exclusively for cutting in the border, there is no reason why plants that occasionally provide a few blooms for the house cannot be incorporated. Place them in different parts of the border so that no one area is denuded after you have raided it for a bunch of flowers, and plant them where they are not too difficult to reach. Try to arrange the planting so that there are always a few flowers to cut.

GROWING CUT FLOWERS

Those plants that will be cut only occasionally can be grown in the normal manner, but those grown especially for cutting may well need special attention. They will need staking to ensure they stay upright and retain their straight stems. They will need protection against pests that may spoil the blooms: earwigs, slugs and aphids are three common pests to many plants. With many cut flowers, sweet peas (*Lathyrus odoratus*) for example, it is important to cut regularly and to remove any dead flowers as this will encourage the plant to continue producing new and reasonably sized blooms. To grow especially large blooms, it may be necessary to remove some of the buds to allow the remaining ones to develop to their full potential.

PLANTS FOR CUTTING

Agrostemma githago (corn cockle)
Amaranthus caudatus (love-lies-bleeding)
Antirrhinum majus (snapdragon)
Brachycome iberidifolia (Swan River daisy)
Calendula officinalis (pot marigold)
Callistephus chinensis (China aster)
Campanula medium (Canterbury bells)
Centaurea (syn. *Amberboa*) *moschata* (sweet sultan)
Chrysanthemum coronarium
Consolida ambigua, syn. *C. ajacis* (larkspur)
Coreopsis (tickseed)
Dianthus barbatus (sweet William)
Dianthus chinensis (China pink)
Digitalis purpurea (foxglove)
Gaillardia pulchella (blanket flower)
Gilia capitata

Godetia
Gypsophila elegans
Helianthus annuus (sunflower)
Iberis amara
Lathyrus odoratus (sweet pea)
Lavatera trimestris (tree mallow)
Limonium sinuatum
Matthiola (stock)
Moluccella laevis (bells of Ireland)
Nicotiana (tobacco plant)
Nigella damascena (love-in-a-mist)
Reseda odorata (mignonette)
Rudbeckia hirta (coneflower)
Salvia farinacea
Salpiglossis
Scabiosa atropurpurea (sweet scabious)
Tagetes erecta (African marigold)
Tagetes patula (French marigold)
Tithonia rotundifolia (Mexican sunflower)
Zinnia elegans

CUTTING ANNUALS

1 Regular cutting helps to ensure a continuing supply of new flowers. If any of the flowers are allowed to run to seed, vital energy that would otherwise be channelled into producing new blooms is used up. Removing dead flowers and any developing seed helps to conserve this energy.

2 The best time to cut flowers is just as they are opening or about to open. Cut the longest available stalk, which can be trimmed back later if necessary. Plunge the cut flowers up to their necks in lukewarm water and store them in a cool shady place for a few hours before you arrange them in a vase or jug.

3 The length of time that a cut flower stays fresh and attractive varies from variety to variety. This period can be extended by adding a proprietary cut-flower food to the water at the dosage recommended on the packet.

4 Before placing in a vase cut the stems to the required length and remove all leaves that would be below water when arranged. The style of the arrangement is up to you – experiment with different combinations, and use your imagination!

5 The finished vase will make the effort of raising and growing the plants worth while. The best place for cut flowers is in a cool, airy position away from direct sunlight.

Above: *Dahlias make excellent cut flowers and can be grown in a general border, as here, or in a separate plot, especially for cutting. This variety is 'Aylett's Gaiety'.*

Annuals for Drying

Drying annuals prolongs their useful life, allowing them to be used as decoration for a second year or even longer. (Do not keep them too long, though; there is nothing sadder than faded, dusty dried flowers.) A number of annuals are grown specifically for drying, but it is surprising how many ordinary annuals can also be effectively dried. As well as display, many can be used as components of a pot-pourri, either for their colour or their fragrance.

GROWING FOR DRYING

Annuals that are grown specifically for drying are probably best grown in separate rows, especially if they are needed in quantity. Those that are used to just add a bit of variety to an arrangement and therefore are needed in small quantities only can be grown in ordinary borders.

DRYING

There are several different ways in which to dry annuals, but air-drying is the simplest, the cheapest and in many ways the most effective.

The best time for harvesting flowers for drying is on a dry day after any early morning dew or overnight rain has evaporated. The exact time that a flower needs to be picked varies from variety to variety, but generally the best time is soon after it has opened, or in some cases while it is still in bud. You might like to include some buds in your final dried-flower arrangement.

Cut the stems cleanly with a pair of secateurs (pruners), leaving as long a stem as possible. Strip off the lower foliage, leaving bare stems. Place the stems in small bunches and bind them with rubber bands, raffia or string. The advantage of rubber bands is that they contract to take up the shrinkage that takes place as the stems dry. If carelessly tied with string the bunch may come loose, scattering the flowers and possibly damaging them.

Hang the bunches upside down in a warm, airy place. Avoid hanging them where they are in direct sunlight or anywhere where the air is liable to be damp. The ideal place is in a warm kitchen, away from any steaming kettles or pans. As well as being practical, drying flowers in the kitchen can also be very decorative. An airing cupboard is another perfect place.

The flowers are ready to use when they are completely dried. Check the thickest part of the flower or stem, breaking one if necessary to test it.

Individual flowers for use on home-made greetings cards or bookmarks for giving as gifts can be dried by pressing with a heavy weight between sheets of blotting paper or by burying them in silica gel crystals.

Right: *Cornflowers* (Centaurea cyanus) *are valuable as they add the colour blue to the dried-flower arranger's palette.*

FLOWERS FOR DRYING

Ageratum (floss flower)
Amaranthus caudatus (love-lies-bleeding)
Ammobium alatum
Atriplex hortensis
Briza maxima (greater quaking grass)
Briza minor (lesser quaking grass)
Calendula officinalis (pot marigold)
Celosia argentea
Celosia cristata
Centaurea cyanus (cornflower)
Centaurea (syn. *Amberboa*) *moschata* (sweet sultan)
Clarkia
Consolida ambigua, syn. *C. ajacis* (larkspur)
Gilia capitata
Gomphrena globosa
Gypsophila elegans
Helichrysum bracteatum, syn. *Bracteantha bracteata* (everlasting flower)

Helipterum roseum (syn. *Acroclinium roseum*)
Hordeum jubatum (squirrel tail grass)
Lagurus ovatus (hare's-tail grass)
Limonium sinuatum
Lunaria annua (honesty)
Moluccella laevis (bells of Ireland)
Nicandra physalodes (apple of Peru, shoo-fly)
Nigella damascena (love-in-a-mist)
Onopordum acanthium (Scotch thistle)
Salvia horminum (syn. *S. viridis*)
Scabiosa atropurpurea (sweet scabious)
Setaria italica (foxtail millet, Italian millet)
Stipa pennata
Tagetes erecta (African marigold)

Above: *Pot marigolds (*Calendula officinalis*) tend to shrivel slightly when dried but are good because of their strong orange colour.*

Right: *The bells of Ireland (*Moluccella laevis*) dry to a pale green that soon changes to soft cream.*

Above: Limonium sinuatum *is one of the classic plants for drying. It can be grown, as here, as part of a border, but is often grown separately, especially for cutting and drying.*

Finding the Right Annual

There is a tremendous range of colours in annual plants, so wide that with a little thought and imagination you can paint any picture you like.

USING COLOURS

Each colour has many tones and shades, and annuals reflect all the possible nuances. On the whole, though, most annuals are of a bright nature and this must be taken into account when using them.

Since so many annuals come from hot, Mediterranean-type climates, they often have bright colours, which are necessary in harsh, bright light for attracting passing pollinators. Many gardeners take advantage of this, using annuals to provide strong impact in the garden. A sudden splash of bright red pelargoniums or salvias, for example, will always catch the eye. However, bright colours are not always easy to combine as they may clash with one another or create a confused picture in which there is nowhere for the eye to rest. Hot, vibrant colours can get lost in the hurly-burly of a mixed border and tend to look better when used as part of a design for bedding plants. They can look even better when used to enliven the façade of a building, possibly in window boxes or hanging baskets. This is where bright pelargoniums and trailing petunias come into their own.

Many annuals, nonetheless, are subtly coloured and can be combined to create a more romantic image. The misty blues of love-in-a-mist (*Nigella damascena*), the soft, silky pinks of lavateras, the smoky lavenders of some of the opium poppies (*Papaver somniferum*), or the apricots of *Collomia grandiflora* can be used singly in drifts or combined to form a restful image.

COMBINING COLOURS

Some colours mix better than others. Near neighbours on the artist's colour wheel combine together much more sympathetically than the contrasting colours that are opposite each other. Thus, red flowers merge seamlessly with purple ones, but orange will stand out quite starkly against blue. Combining colours can be used to great effect, but try to avoid creating a restless image as a result of combining too many colours at once. Drifts of colour are much easier on the eye.

When you grow plants from seed you can use particular colour strains which are almost guaranteed to come true. However, if you buy mixed seed, the plants could turn out to be any colour and this must be borne in mind when planting them out. Similarly, when you buy seedlings from a garden centre or nursery it may be a good idea to see at least some in flower before you buy to ensure you get what you want. Your carefully planned scheme could be ruined by a wishy-washy pink appearing where you expected a strong yellow.

Left: *A lot of careful thought needs to be given to colourful bedding schemes like this. Drawing them out on a piece of graph paper with coloured pencils helps with planning – it can be an enjoyable way to pass a winter evening.*

Above: *Foliage plays an important part in any colour scheme. Here the delicate pink of this opium poppy (*Papaver somniferum*) is beautifully set off against the grey leaves.*

Above: *Sweet peas (*Lathyrus odoratus*) come in a wide range of colours and can be mixed, as here, or grown separately.*

Left: *One of the benefits of modern breeding methods is the consistency in colour that can be produced. Here the French marigold, Tagetes patula 'Aurora Primrose', produces a batch of identical flowers.*

Red

Red has two faces: one is tinged with orange and the other with blue. The orange reds are hot colours and combine well with oranges and golden and orange yellows. On the other hand, the blue reds are more subdued but often richer, more velvety in tone and combine well with purples, violets and blues. The flame reds are exciting, while the blue reds are more sophisticated.

ORANGE REDS

Although there are times when the two groups of red can be used together, they generally do not mix in a pleasing way and so tend to be kept separate. Use orange reds where you want to inject some vibrancy and excitement into your garden designs, whether it be in beds and borders or in hanging baskets and other containers. But remember that, like parties, too much of a good thing can become monotonous after a while. Use hot strong colours sparingly, but when you do, make them tell.

Hot reds have the advantage of appearing to draw nearer than they really are, and show up well at a distance. This is one of the reasons why they are so good on the façades of buildings. For example, even a single geranium will stand out in a window box on a third-floor windowsill. A pale lavender flower would be invisible.

BLUE REDS

Blue reds can be used more extensively than orange reds as they are less intense. Unfortunately, as far as annuals are concerned plant breeders obviously feel that gardeners prefer the hot, flame reds as these are by far in the majority. However, purple reds now seem to be amongst the most popular colours of the trailing petunias, and hanging baskets filled with these seem to add a touch of richness to a building.

Below: *Reds can vary in their intensity but this* Verbena *'Sandy Scarlet' is as intense and brightly coloured as they come – it is positively dazzling and makes a great contribution to any bed.*

POPULAR RED ANNUALS

Adonis aestivalis
Alcea rosea 'Scarlet'
Amaranthus caudatus (love-lies-bleeding)
Antirrhinum 'Scarlet Giant' (snapdragon)
Begonia semperflorens 'Lucifer'
Begonia semperflorens 'Volcano'
Cleome spinosa (syn. *C. hassleriana*) 'Cherry Queen'
Cosmos bipinnatus 'Pied Piper Red'
Dianthus chinensis 'Fire Carpet'
Impatiens (busy Lizzie) Impact Scarlet
Impatiens 'Super Elfin Red'
Impatiens 'Tempo Burgundy'
Impatiens 'Tempo Scarlet'
Lathyrus odoratus 'Airwarden'
Lathyrus odoratus 'Winston Churchill'
Linum grandiflorum
Lobelia erinus 'Red Cascade'
Lobelia erinus 'Rosamund'
Malope trifida 'Vulcan'
Nicotiana 'Crimson'
Papaver rhoeas (field poppy)
Pelargonium (many red varieties)
Petunia 'Mirage Velvet'
Petunia 'Red Star'
Petunia 'Scarlet'
Salvia splendens
Tagetes patula 'Cinnabar'
Tagetes patula 'Red Marietta'
Tagetes patula 'Scarlet Sophie'
Tropaeolum majus 'Empress of India'
Verbena 'Blaze'
Verbena 'Defiance'
Verbena 'Sandy Scarlet'
Verbena 'Sparkle'

Above: *Dahlias produce some very rich reds indeed, but few are as vivid as this 'Bishop of Llandaff' with its flame-red flowers.*

Above: *Pelargoniums are available in a wide range of striking reds, varying from orange red, through scarlet to crimson as well as the more purple reds.*

Right: *A plant that produces consistently good red flowers is the busy Lizzie (Impatiens). It is a valuable low-growing plant for painting swathes of red in a bedding sheme.*

Pink

Pink is a very useful colour in the annual spectrum. It is obviously not as bright as the reds but it can still be quite bright and even startling and brash, particularly when mixed with a tinge of purple and moving more towards cerise and magenta shades. On the other hand pink can be very soft and romantic. You have to be careful in choosing the right colour for the effect you want to get. If possible see the plant in flower first.

USING PINK

Generally, pinks are considered soft colours and are mixed with similar tones. They tend to mix best with lavenders and soft blues. But they can be used with reds to tone them down a bit. Pinks do not mix harmoniously with bright yellows and oranges.

Pink-coloured annuals can be used in a wide range of garden situations, from hanging baskets and window boxes to bedding schemes or perhaps mixed in with perennials. They look particularly good in containers, especially stone or stone-coloured ones.

POPULAR PINK ANNUALS

Agrostemma githago 'Milas'
Alcea rosea 'Rose'
Antirrhinum majus (snapdragon – numerous pink varieties)
Argyranthemum (syn. *Chrysanthemum*) *frutescens* 'Mary Wootton'
Begonia semperflorens 'Pink Avalanche'
Callistephus chinensis (China aster)
Centaurea cyanus (cornflower – pink forms)
Crepis rubra
Dianthus (carnation, pink – various varieties)
Diascia (numerous varieties)
Godetia grandiflora 'Satin Pink'
Helichrysum bracteatum (syn. *Bracteantha bracteata*) 'Rose'
Helipterum roseum (syn. *Acroclinium roseum*)
Impatiens (busy Lizzie) 'Impact Rose'
Impatiens 'Super Elfin Rose'
Impatiens 'Tempo Blush'
Lathyrus odoratus (sweet pea – numerous pink varieties)
Lavatera trimestris 'Mont Rose'
Lavatera trimestris 'Pink Beauty'
Lavatera trimestris 'Silver Cup'
Malope trifida 'Pink Queen'
Matthiola (stock – numerous varieties)
Nicotiana 'Domino Salmon-Pink'
Nigella damascena 'Miss Jekyll Pink'
Papaver somniferum (opium poppy)
Pelargonium (many pink varieties)
Petunia (numerous pink varieties)
Silene coeli-rosa 'Rose Angel'
Silene pendula 'Peach Blossom'
Verbena 'Amour Light Pink'

Above: *This is a spectacular mass planting of* Osteospermum *'Lady Leitrim', whose flowers grow pinker as they age. They create an informal meadow-like effect planted in this way.*

Above: *There is really nothing to surpass the delicate paper-tissue flowers of the opium poppy* (Papaver somniferum) *– it produces some of the most soft and subtle pinks for the annual border.*

Above: Oenothera speciosa *'Rosea' produces a profusion of delicate pink flowers. The species form,* O. speciosa, *known as white evening primrose, has white flowers that turn pink as they age, creating a delightful effect.*

Above: *Foxgloves (*Digitalis*) create wonderfully elegant spires of flowers, bringing height to a planting scheme. These flowers vary in colour from a light pink to purple and look very statuesque in the border.*

Left: Cleome spinosa *(syn.* C. hassleriana) *looks like a firework sending off sparks in all directions. The flower buds are dark pink, fading as they open.*

Above: *Cosmos flowers over a long period and comes in a wide range of colours. There are several pinks including this lovely dark one, 'Versailles Tetra'.*

Blue and Lavender

Blue can be that bright, clean-cut colour that has a great intensity or it can be softened to such an extent that it only has a whisper of colour left, creating a very soft, hazy image. Intense blues can be used in a bold way in the garden, but the softer blues are good for romantic container arrangements, especially those in large stone pots or urns.

USING BLUES

Blues are versatile and can be combined with most colours. They create a rather rich, luxurious combination with purple reds, but avoid mixing them with orange reds. With orange, however, the effects can be startling, so use this combination sparingly, otherwise it becomes overpowering and rather tedious to look at.

Blue and yellow is another exciting combination. These colours, which are near opposites on the artist's colour wheel, form a fresh, clean-looking contrast. Pale blues and yellows are more hazy and have a softer, more romantic image, but still retain a distinctive fresh quality, much more distinct than, say, soft blues and pinks.

Lavenders combined with pinks are a wonderfully romantic combination. Although they can look washed out in

bright light, they can look wonderful in a grey, northern atmosphere. Blues set against silver or grey foliage create an interesting combination that is severe yet soft.

*Right: The beautifully intricate annual love-in-a-mist (*Nigella damascena*) is typically a delicate light blue. However, love-in-a-mist is now available in a wider range of colours including dark blue. The impact of the blue petals is further enhanced by the elegant ruff of green filigree foliage.*

POPULAR BLUE AND LAVENDER ANNUALS

Ageratum houstonianum
Borago officinalis (borage)
Brachycome iberidifolia (Swan River daisy)
Campanula medium (Canterbury bells)
Centaurea cyanus (cornflower)
Consolida ambigua, syn. *C. ajacis* (larkspur)
Cynoglossum amabile
Echium 'Blue Bedder'
Echium vulgare
Felicia bergeriana (kingfisher daisy)
Gilia

Lathyrus odoratus (sweet pea – various varieties)
Limonium sinuatum 'Azure'
Limonium sinuatum 'Blue Bonnet'
Lobelia erinus
Myosotis (forget-me-not)
Nemophila menziesii (baby blue-eyes)
Nigella damascena (love-in-a-mist)
Nigella hispanica
Nolana paradoxa 'Blue Bird'
Petunia (some varieties)
Primula (blue varieties)
Salvia farinacea 'Victoria'

Above: *The delightful* Galactites tomentosa *is a non-troublesome thistle that produces light purple flowers. These look wonderfully striking against the variegated foliage. This is a particularly good plant for including in the mixed border.*

Above right: *Ageratums make perfect bedding plants with their small powder-puff flower heads that last throughout the summer and well into the autumn. This rich reddish-purple variety is 'North Star'.*

Right: Brachycome iberidifolia, *the Swan River daisy, comes in a variety of shades that range from blue to violet and even include rich purple.*

White and Cream

White flowers are very fashionable. Long associated with purity, peace and tranquillity, they are much in demand for wedding bouquets and as cut flowers. The purity and clarity of white gives it a touch of class and sophistication that other colours can rarely match. Cream is white with a little yellow added. It is a more sensuous, luxurious colour, and lacks the more clinical qualities of pure white.

USING WHITE

White is a good colour for brightening up a planting scheme or container display and can be used to illuminate dark corners of the garden. White busy Lizzies, for example, in a hanging basket against a dark background or in shade will shine out. White also has a magical quality as the light fades in the evening, standing out long after other colours have disappeared in the gloom. This makes it an excellent choice for use in containers and other displays, especially in areas where you sit in the evening.

White will mix well with other colours, although it can sometimes be a little too stark in contrast with some. Cream will often blend in more sympathetically, especially with colours on the orange-red side of the colour spectrum.

One big drawback with white flowers is that they so often refuse to die gracefully. Once they have finished flowering you are left with shrivelled brown petals that stand out far too well against the remaining white flowers. To keep such displays at their best, it is essential to deadhead at least once a day.

POPULAR WHITE AND CREAM ANNUALS

Alcea rosea (hollyhock – white varieties)
Antirrhinum 'White Wonder'
Argyranthemum (syn. *Chrysanthemum*) *frutescens* (white varieties)
Centaurea (syn. *Amberboa*) *moschata* 'The Bride' (sweet sultan)
Clarkia pulchella 'Snowflake'
Cleome spinosa (syn. *C. hassleriana*) 'Helen Campbell'
Consolida ambigua (syn. *C. ajacis*) 'Imperial White King'
Cosmos bipinnatus 'Purity'
Dianthus (carnation, pink – various varieties)
Digitalis purpurea alba (white foxglove)
Eschscholzia californica 'Milky White'
Eustoma grandiflorum (white varieties)
Gypsophila elegans 'Giant White'
Helianthus annuus 'Italian White'
Helichrysum bracteatum (syn. *Bracteantha bracteata*) 'White'
Hibiscus trionum (flower-of-the-hour)
Iberis amara
Impatiens (busy Lizzie) Super Elfin White
Lathyrus odoratus (sweet pea – various varieties)
Lavatera trimestris 'Mont Blanc'
Limonium sinuatum 'Iceberg'
Lobelia erinus 'Snowball'
Lobularia maritima, syn. *Alyssum maritimum* (sweet sultan)
Malope trifida 'Alba'
Matthiola (stock – white varieties)
Nemesia 'Mello White'
Nemophila maculata
Nicotiana alata, syn. *N. affinis* (tobacco plant)
Nicotiana sylvestris
Nolana paradoxa 'Snowbird'
Omphalodes linifolia
Osteospermum 'Glistening White'
Papaver somniferum (opium poppy – white varieties)
Pelargonium (various white forms)
Petunia (various white forms)
Tripleurospermum inodora 'Bridal Robe'
Viola × wittrockiana (pansy – white varieties)

Left: *The tender perennial Osteospermum 'Prostratum' is a lovely pure white, but it needs plenty of sun, as the flowers only open in sunlight.*

Right: *Cream is a good colour to combine with a wide range of other colours, especially schemes planted with hot yellows and orange reds. The marigold Tagetes 'French Vanilla' demonstrates clearly the true beauty of this colour.*

Above: Iberis crenata *is rather more lax than other species of candytuft, and produces an abundance of stunning white flowers. These emerge from the mauve buds that are still held in the centre of the flower head.*

Above: *Many flowers also have white forms including this foxglove,* Digitalis purpurea alba.

Above: *For ethereal, billowing clouds of white flowers it is hard to beat* Gypsophila, *which brings an elegant tracery to a planting scheme. This annual form is* G. elegans *'White Elephant'.*

Above: *The old-fashioned annual* Collomia grandiflora *produces beautiful flowers at the height of summer that are the most wonderful peach-cream colour.*

Yellow and Gold

There are three distinct colours within the yellow part of the artist's colour spectrum, all exhibiting different qualities in a planting scheme. One side is tinged with green and may be described as a cool colour, while the other side is tinged with orange, making it very much a hot colour. In between are the pure, clear yellows. The orange yellows as well as pure gold have a warm, cosy feeling about them, whereas the greener yellows are much fresher and cleaner looking. The pure, clear yellows make a tremendous impact and attract the eye more readily than most other colours. Yellow is also a stimulating colour. For this reason, yellow flowers are often planted in gardens outside hospices where people come for healing.

POPULAR YELLOW AND GOLD ANNUALS

Alcea rosea 'Yellow'
Anoda cristata 'Buttercup'
Antirrhinum majus (snapdragon – yellow varieties)
Argemone mexicana (Mexican poppy)
Argyranthemum (syn. *Chrysanthemum*) *frutescens* 'Jamaica Primrose'
Calendula officinalis 'Kablouna'
Chrysanthemum segetum
Coreopsis 'Sunray'
Glaucium flavum (horned poppy)
Helianthus annuus (sunflower)
Limnanthes douglasii (poached egg plant)
Limonium sinuatum 'Goldcoast'
Lonas annua
Mentzelia lindleyi
Mimulus (creeping zinnia – various varieties)
Sanvitalia procumbens
Tagetes (marigold – yellow varieties)
Tropaeolum majus (Indian cress)
Tropaeolum peregrinum, syn. *T. canariense* (canary creeper)
Viola × wittrockiana (pansy – yellow varieties)

USING YELLOWS

The three colours are often used indiscriminately, yet with a bit of care would fit in with their companions far more comfortably. Clear yellow will sit happily with most other colours, purple being the least comfortable combination, although even this contrast can be worthwhile if not overdone.

A bed or container of warm yellows is always welcoming. These cheerful colours go well with flame reds, oranges, creams and buffs, but they can dominate their companions.

The green or lemon yellows look much better when associated with greens, blues and white. They can be gay and bright, but create a fresher effect than the warmer colours.

Right: *The poached egg plant* (Limnanthes douglasii) *is much-loved for its cheerful disposition as well as its ability to self-sow and reappear each year.*

Above: *A self-sowing wallflower that reappears every year without any intervention from the gardener is the delightful* Erysimum helveticum.

Above: *For sheer architectural grandeur there is little to beat the giant spires of mulleins* (Verbascum) *which tower 2m (7ft) or more above the border.*

Above: *Marigolds come in an infinite range of yellows, golds and oranges and even reddy browns. This one is a French marigold called* Tagetes patula *'Golden Gem'.*

Above: *Charming argyranthemums with their daisy-like flowers come in pink and white as well as yellow. Here the golden yellow is set off brilliantly by the dark green of the foliage.*

Above: *Annual chrysanthemums are perhaps not as showy as their perennial cousins, but they can still put on a wonderful display. This one is called* Chrysanthemum tenuiloba *'Golden Fleck'.*

Orange

Orange is a warm, friendly colour. It is predominantly a colour of late summer and autumn, but it is welcome at any time of the year. It has quite a wide range of shades, from deep gold (the lighter golds are closer to yellow) through to almost flame red. At the deeper end of the spectrum, it is a hot colour, exciting and vibrant. At the golden end it is warm rather than hot and can be used a bit more freely.

USING ORANGE

Orange mixes well with most colours although the redder shades are not so complementary with the bluer reds, including purple and pink, unless you like to combine colours that clash. The more yellow colours mix better with blues.

Orange shows up well against green foliage and can be picked out at a distance. It can be used wherever annuals are appropriate and is frequently found in the form of African marigolds (*Tagetes erecta*) and French marigolds (*T. patula*), in large bedding schemes.

Although orange is most widely seen in autumn gardens, not only in flowers such as chrysanthemums but in trees and shrubs with coloured foliage and berries, there are also many annuals that can add a vibrant orange note throughout the year. The winter-flowering pansies (*Viola* × *wittrockiana* Universal Series) include orange varieties which continue flowering into the spring, and wallflowers (*Erysimum*), snapdragons (*Antirrhinum*) and pot marigolds (*Calendula*) then come into their own, the latter often flowering quite early if it has been left to self-sow. During the summer, nasturtiums (*Tropaeolum*) in various shades will follow.

Right: *Although osteospermums have the annoying habit of closing up on dull days, they can still make a splash with their bright colours. This pure orange variety is* O. hyoseroides *'Gaiety'.*

Above: *Cannas can be used to make strong extrovert statements in a bedding scheme. Many have bright orange flowers and this one, 'Roi Humbert', has contrasting purple foliage as an added bonus.*

Above: *Calceolarias have curious slipper-shaped flowers. The bedding varieties come in shades of yellow, orange or red. This bright orange variety is 'Kentish Hero'.*

Mixed Annuals

The flowers of many annuals are not, of course, restricted to a single colour. Each flower may consist of several colours although there may be one basic colour. For example, salpiglossis have dark or differently coloured throats and very prominent veining, which help to disguise or alter the overall appearance of the base colour. This means that flowers that are basically coloured orange will have quite a different effect in a display than totally orange flowers, such as calendula.

USING MIXED COLOURS

Some plants have several colours in their flowers, without any one being dominant, and planning precise colour schemes with this type of flower is very difficult if you are not to avoid a chaotic mixture. This is not to say that they are not worth growing, simply that they have to be handled differently and rather carefully. You must decide what their overall effect is likely to be when used in a specific planting scheme. You should also be careful when mixing them with other plants that have mixed colours as the general effect may become rather uneven and restless. Sometimes it can be effective to echo one of the colours in an adjacent planting.

There is an increasing tendency on the part of seed merchants to market packets of mixed colours rather than just a single one. For instance, some merchants may only have mixed colours of snapdragon (*Antirrhinum*) available. You can sometimes achieve a lovely cottage-garden effect with these mixtures, for example of sweet peas, but if you do want a more planned scheme, check in different catalogues and with

luck you should find the specific colours you want. Surprisingly, it is often the smaller companies that offer a better service in this respect.

A similar problem arises when buying plants from a garden centre or nursery. Sometimes it can be impossible to find the colour you want and you have to make do with a mixture. At other times the packs of plants may not be labelled. Although it is not always a good idea to wait for annuals to flower before buying, it may sometimes be necessary to ensure that you get the right colours.

If you save your own seed, of snapdragons for example, there is no guarantee that the resulting seedlings will be the same colour as the parent from which the seed was collected. This is further complicated by the fact that some plants are more likely to come true than others.

Right: *These marigolds (Tagetes) are two-toned but the colours are relatively close to each other on the colour wheel and so they blend well together giving a harmonious effect.*

POPULAR MIXED ANNUALS

Mixed Colour Annuals	Mixed Colour Seeds Available in Packets
Dianthus barbatus (sweet William	*Alcea rosea* (hollyhock)
Dianthus chinensis (China pink)	*Antirrhinum majus* (snapdragon)
Nemesia	*Callistephus chinensis* (Chinese aster)
Primula	*Cosmos*
Salpiglossis	*Erysimum* (wallflower)
Schizanthus (butterfly flower, poor man's orchid)	*Eschscholzia californica*
Tagetes (marigold)	*Lathyrus odoratus* (sweet pea)
Viola × wittrockiana (pansy)	

Above: *Many flowers change colour as the flowers mature and finally fade. This* Verbena *'Peaches and Cream' goes through several stages.*

Below: *A common coloration is where one colour shades into another. In this pelargonium the dark pink merges into a much softer one.*

Above: *Where two colours are strongly contrasted, as in this nemesia, the overall effect is much more startling and eye-catching.*

Annuals for Foliage

There is a tendency to think of annuals only in terms of their flower-power, but they have a lot more to offer. Indeed, many are useful solely for their foliage, which can be wonderfully coloured, but there are a few that are notable for both their foliage and their flowers. Even plain green foliage often comes in attractive and interesting shapes, setting off the flowers very effectively.

FOLIAGE COLOUR

In annuals, foliage colours are far from being restricted to green. Red orach (*Atriplex hortensis* 'Rubra') has rich purple leaves which go well with pinks and silvers, and it is a marvellous plant for dotting about a mixed border of soft colours. Several silver-foliaged annuals, which are particularly good for setting off blues and pinks, can be used as part of a formal bedding scheme or in a more mixed planting. The statuesque Scotch thistles (*Onopordum acanthium*) are too big for most bedding schemes but they fit well into large borders or stand as individual plants.

As well as these striking single colours, there are some annuals with variegated foliage: *Euphorbia marginata* has a cool white and green combination, while the tender shrub *Abutilon megapotamicum* 'Variegatum' has dark green leaves liberally splashed with gold. *Coleus* (syn. *Solenostemon*), in particular, comes in a wide range of colours and markings, and will often outshine a display of flowers.

OTHER QUALITIES

The shapes of leaves are also of value. The castor-oil plant (*Ricinus communis*), with its large-fingered leaves, for example, is very eye-catching.

The grey or silver leaves of melianthus are also very architecturally shaped.

Scent can add another dimension to interesting foliage. The scented-leaved pelargoniums, for example, come in many varieties with different fragrances, and are delightful in containers positioned where you can crush a leaf as you pass.

Cannas, tender perennials that are usually treated as annuals, have wonderful green or bronze leaves twirled around the stems as well as large brightly coloured flowers. The leaves are large and shiny, which, along with the hot flower colours, adds a touch of the exotic and tropical to any planting scheme.

WINTER

For winter schemes, ornamental cabbages (*Brassica oleracea*) are extremely valuable. The variegated leaves, in shades of pink or white, add a welcome touch of colour at a time when it may be in short supply.

Right: *The beautiful silver of the leaves and the wings on the stems of this* Onopordum acanthium, *or Scotch thistle, gives the plant a stunning appearance. This dramatic shape makes it one of the best architectural plants for beds and borders.*

POPULAR FOLIAGE ANNUALS

Abutilon megapotamicum 'Variegatum'
Ammobium alatum
Atriplex hortensis 'Rubra' (red orach)
Bassia (syn. *Kochia*) *scoparia trichophylla*
Beta vulgaris
Brassica oleracea (ornamental cabbage)
Canna
Coleus blumei (syn. *Solenostemon scutellarioides*)
Euphorbia marginata
Galactites tomentosa
Helichrysum petiolare
Impatiens (busy Lizzie – bronze-leaf forms)
Melianthus major (honeybush)
Ocimum basilicum 'Purple Ruffles'
Onopordum acanthium (Scotch thistle)
Pelargonium (geranium – scented-leaved forms)
Perilla frutescens
Ricinus communis (castor-oil plant)
Senecio cineraria (syn. *S. maritima*)
Silybum marianum
Tropaeolum majus 'Alaska'

Above: Helichrysum petiolare *is a tender perennial that is frequently used in both containers and bedding schemes, mainly for its furry, silvery-grey foliage.*

Above: *A favourite plant for self-sowing is the purple-leaved red orach (*Atriplex hortensis *'Rubra'). It looks best in a position in which the sun can shine through and light up the leaves.*

Right: *The red markings on this unusual and very striking annual,* Medicago echinus, *combine beautifully with the perennial* Geranium phaeum *'Samabor'.*

Annual Grasses

Annual grasses are not as popular as they deserve to be, possibly because in many people's minds annuals are synonymous with flowers, and grasses, perhaps, are associated with lawns. Ornamental grasses do have flowers but they are hardly brightly coloured things when compared with busy Lizzies (*Impatiens*) or pelargoniums. However, grasses have their own subtle charm, and are extremely useful for adding a quietening note to a scheme and for the swaying elegance they bring to mixed borders.

POPULAR ANNUAL GRASSES

Agrostis nebulosa	*Lamarckia aurea* (golden top)
Briza maxima (greater quaking grass)	*Panicum capillare* (old-witch grass)
Briza minor (lesser quaking grass)	*Pennisetum setaceum* (African fountain grass)
Hordeum jubatum (squirreltail grass)	*Pennisetum villosum* (feather top)
Lagurus ovatus (hare's-tail grass)	*Sorghum nigrum*
	Zea mays (ornamental maize)

NATURAL GRACE

What grasses lack in colour they more than make up for in grace and beauty. They have elegant shapes; whether they are tall and wispy or stout clumps, grasses always exhibit the same kind of linear form. The leaves are long and straight. The flower stems are also long and narrow, and even in short grasses are usually taller than the leaves. Even the flowerheads tend to be long and narrow, but if they are spreading then the individual components are narrow, creating a wonderfully diffuse effect.

The numerous flower stems erupt like fountains, taking the eye with them and giving the display an upward thrust. At the same time their simplicity means that there is something cool about grasses. They move gracefully in the slightest breeze. They are gentle, even soothing to the eye, especially after the hurly-burly of conventional, colourful annuals.

USING GRASSES

Grasses can be used by themselves to create a distinct feature or they can be mixed in with other annuals. You are most likely to use them as a whole bedding scheme or as part of one, although they can also be grown in containers, particularly the taller ones. Generally, they are not much use in hanging baskets, but some of the arching types can be effective if used with care.

Most grasses are extremely good at catching the sunlight and can look superb when lit from behind. Place them so that they are between the viewer and the evening sun for some of the most stunning effects. Squirrel-tail grass (*Hordeum jubatum*), for example, creates a wonderful arching, feathery effect, and looks fantastic when it catches the sunlight.

Unfortunately, most of the annual grasses are quite short, although ornamental maize (*Zea mays*) will grow up to 2.4m (8ft) in a season, which is tall enough for most purposes. Most annual grasses have green leaves, but some have a distinct bronze tinge, while others, including ornamental maize, are variegated.

Many annual grasses can be dried and used as indoor decoration. Hare's-tail grass (*Lagurus ovatus*), which has chunky but very soft heads, is a popular drying grass. The feather top (*Pennisetum villosum*), strictly a perennial but a tender one, has more open heads, but again is wonderfully silky.

Below: *Soft grasses look very effective when they are backlit by sunlight, as this squirreltail grass* (Hordeum jubatum) *shows. Stirred by the breeze the effect is even more enchanting.*

Above: *Not all grasses associate well with flowering plants, but in this planting scheme squirreltail grass* (Hordeum jubatum) *makes a very effective partner for* Dahlia *'Yelno Harmony'*.

Above: *Arching grasses have a pleasing, often restful, effect. Here the tender perennial* Pennisetum setaceum *'Cupreum Compactum' adds a tranquil note, in contrast to more colourful plants.*

Above: *Many grasses are useful for drying as well as creating a decorative effect in the garden. The hare's-tail grass* (Lagurus ovatus) *is one such plant.*

Annuals in Pots and Planters

In the past annuals were mainly used as bedding plants in borders, but with the increased interest in container planting, including hanging baskets and window boxes, annuals have taken on a new lease of life, and they make the most perfect container plants.

USING ANNUALS

Containers are an immediate way of gardening, almost like flower arranging except that the flowers have roots. One minute the pot is empty, the next it is full of flowers. Annuals lend themselves to this style of gardening. They have such a short life cycle that they flower very early in their lives, soon after planting out, or they may already be in flower when planted.

Many have a long flowering period, often covering the whole of the summer and most of the autumn as well. They are also colourful, a factor that most people want in their containers. An added bonus is that they are relatively easy to look after: they just need watering and a bit of dead-heading.

Almost any annuals can be used in containers, though the very tall ones will usually be less successful. Scotch thistles (*Onopordum acanthium*), for example, would look out of proportion in a small pot, but could be effective in the centre of a large arrangement.

CONTAINERS

Containers can be used singly or in groups. An advantage of containers is that they can be moved around. Groups can be reformed or split up, constantly changing the scene. If one pot begins to look a bit straggly or the flowers fade, then it can be moved out of sight and perhaps another used to replace it. Collect as many different types and sizes of container as you can and use them imaginatively.

PLANTING TECHNIQUES

When planting a container, you will have to add crocks to the bottom in order to aid drainage. Plants in containers need plenty of water, but they do not like sitting in stagnant water, so it is important to ensure that any excess water can drain away easily. The compost (soil mix) can be either a general one or one that has been especially formulated for use in pots and other containers.

As care and attention are usually lavished on containers by way of daily watering and regular feeding, you can pack plants more tightly than you normally would in a bed or border. Keep the plants neat by removing dead heads and any straggly growths. The perfectionist always has a few spare plants tucked away out of sight to use as replacements if one of the plants in the container dies or begins to flag.

Left: An evergreen cordyline has been livened up for the summer by the addition of colourful annuals. As the flowers die, different ones can replace them according to the seasons. For example, winter pansies are good plants to add interest to an evergreen shrub as they bloom non-stop right through the gloomier months and are not particularly affected by the weather.

Below: As this lovely container planting shows, there is nothing to beat the striking combination of pink and purple flowers with silver foliage.

PLANTING CONTAINERS WITH ANNUALS

1 Before you start to plant, assemble all the materials you need: a container, crocks, perhaps a stone, compost (soil mix), water-retaining crystals, slow-release fertilizer, and your chosen plants and a trowel if you are using one. Pots can be heavy when they are filled with wet compost, so it is best to fill them where they are to be sited.

2 Ensure the container has drainage holes. Partially cover any large holes with an irregularly shaped stone, to prevent the compost (soil mix) falling out, then place other crocks in the bottom of the container to aid drainage.

3 Nearly fill the container with compost (soil mix) and add water-retaining crystals, following the manufacturer's instructions. Compost in containers dries out very quickly and these help reduce the amount of watering required. They swell up into a jelly-like substance, enabling the compost to retain much more water than it normally would.

4 Constant watering washes away many of the nutrients in the compost (soil mix) before the plants can take them up, so it is important to feed them regularly. Adding a slow-release fertilizer to the compost before planting provides food for several months, so you do not have to apply liquid feed regularly.

5 Fill the container with compost (soil mix) almost to the top and gently firm down. Make planting holes using a trowel or your hand and insert the plants to the same depth as they were in their pots or trays. Once all the plants are in position, firm and tidy up the compost, then water well.

6 Tidy up the container by cutting off any damaged stems. Tease out the stems to make the plants look natural and as if they have been planted for some time.

7 The finished container will look even more effective if grouped together with others. Remember to water containers regularly: even in winter, sun and wind can be quite drying, and in a hot summer they may need watering more than once a day.

Annuals in Window Boxes

By making use of wall space, window boxes allow for vertical gardening. This is particularly important where ground space is restricted, but it also helps to create a three-dimensional garden. Also, they are useful for transforming what otherwise may be a rather dull building or wall.

SAFETY
Window boxes are heavy when filled with moist soil, so if the site is windy and exposed, it is important that they are fixed securely. A falling window box is not only a broken and wasted window box, but it is extremely dangerous to anyone underneath. If you do not feel competent to fix it, ask a professional to do the job; it will be cheaper than any possible litigation resulting from a window box falling on someone's head.

MATERIALS
Window boxes are made of various different materials. Terracotta and replica stone look good but are heavy. Plastic ones usually look what they are, but they are lightweight and if covered with trailing plants cannot be seen. Wood is a compromise; it looks good and is reasonably lightweight, but it will eventually rot. Wood's big advantage is that the box can be tailor-made to fit the space.

PLANTS FOR WINDOW BOXES
The range of plants for window boxes is more limited than for pots. Choose a few upright, bushy plants for the rear and trailing ones for the front. For winter and spring use, it is often a good idea to use a few dwarf conifers or evergreen shrubs to give the box structure. You can also do this for summer, but with so many varieties of plants at your disposal it is not so necessary.

PLANTING TECHNIQUES
Place crocks in the bottom of the box to allow easy drainage. There are specially formulated composts (soil or planting mixes) for window boxes, but a general compost is usually more than adequate. Set the plants close together so that when they are in full growth no soil shows; a thinly planted window box can look rather sad and messy.

Keep the box well watered; every day is likely to be necessary. A special pump-action water dispenser with a long nozzle can be used to water them from the ground, but higher ones have to be watered from the window (site the box well below the window so that it will open) or from a ladder. Exercise caution if you use a ladder.

POSITIONING WINDOW BOXES
The obvious place for a window box is outside a window, but their shape and size means that they are suited to other positions. They are good for placing on the top of walls, for example, or on the ground, perhaps together with round pots.

POPULAR ANNUALS FOR WINDOWBOXES

Ageratum (floss flower)
Antirrhinum (snapdragon)
Begonia
Bidens
Brachycome
Cerinthe
Chrysanthemum
Dianthus (carnation, pink)
Echium
Felicia
Fuchsia
Helichrysum
Impatiens (busy Lizzie)
Laurentia (syn. *Isotoma*)
Lobelia
Myosotis (forget-me-not)
Nicotiana (tobacco plant)
Pelargonium (geranium)
Petunia
Sanvitalia
Schizanthus (butterfly flower, poor man's orchid)
Senecio
Tagetes (marigold)
Tropaeolum (nasturtium)
Viola × wittrockiana (pansy)

Above: *Cheerful-looking pansies and lobelias are excellent plants for window boxes because they last for a long time and are very little trouble. Some varieties of pansy can also be used for winter displays. As this trough shows, long, box-like containers can be used successfully on the ground as well as on windowsills.*

PLANTING A WINDOW BOX WITH ANNUALS

1 Assemble all the ingredients: these include a window box, irregularly shaped stones, good quality compost (soil mix), water-retaining crystals, slow-release fertilizer, plants and a trowel if you are using one. If the box is light, assemble it on the ground. If it is heavy, make it up in position, especially if it is to be fixed high up.

2 Stagnant water can be a problem in inadequately drained boxes, so always buy, or make, boxes with holes in the bottom. Place irregularly shaped stones over the bottom of the box to help water drain down towards the holes. Partially cover the holes with these to stop compost (soil mix) falling through.

3 Partially fill the box with compost (soil mix), then mix in water-retaining crystals following the manufacturer's instructions. Continue to fill the box with compost, then gently firm down.

4 Make planting holes with a trowel or your hand and insert the plants to the same depths as they were in their pots or trays. Since you will be constantly watering and feeding the plants, it is possible to plant much more closely together than you would in open ground.

5 Since the window box will be watered frequently, the nutrients in the compost (soil mix) will quickly get washed away, so regular feeding is very important. This is traditionally done by adding a liquid feed to the water every week or so. Alternatively, slow-release fertilizer can be added, either in tablet form, as shown here, or as granules mixed into the compost (soil mix) before planting. Both of these should supply sufficient food for the season.

6 Water the window box thoroughly. The box still looks under-filled, but the plants will soon grow and spread out to fill the whole box. If it is possible to plant a box away from its final position, it can be filled with plants and left for a while until they are all in full flower before being displayed.

7 Boxes that are heavier than this one should be filled in position so that they do not have to be carried and lifted. As well as avoiding physical damage to the gardener, it also prevents the plants being damaged in transit.

Annuals in Hanging Baskets

Hanging baskets are ever increasing in popularity and seed merchants and plant suppliers are constantly searching out new annuals to feed demand. There are now so many bushy and trailing plants to choose from, you can really let your imagination run riot. There is even a trailing variety of tomato, 'Tumbler', which not only looks attractive but provides the added bonus of a crop of delicious fruit.

Above: *Hanging baskets like this can be very heavy so make sure that the fixing point is strong enough. Check each year that it is still secure before replanting the hanging basket.*

THE BASKETS

Baskets consist of three parts: the basket, a liner and a support, frequently a chain. The baskets are usually made from plastic-coated wire. Increasingly they are also available in just plastic but these do not look as good (if you can see them under the plants) and can become brittle.

Liners can be made of compressed paper, coir (coconut fibre) matting or moss. Moss is the most natural-looking but stocks in the wild are being threatened by over-collecting. Paper is recycled and coir is cultivated, so both of these are environmentally acceptable.

You can use either a good general-purpose compost (soil mix) or a specially formulated hanging-basket compost which includes water-retaining gel or crystals. In this case, do not add further gel or crystals, as excessive quantities would cause problems when they expand.

PLANTING HANGING BASKETS

Most hanging baskets include tender annuals so they cannot be placed outside until after the last frosts, but they can be made up in advance and left indoors until the danger of frosts has passed, by which time the basket will have filled out and with luck be in full flower.

Plant the hanging basket tightly so that there are few spaces between the plants. This is acceptable as there should be no shortage of moisture and nutrients if the basket is regularly watered and fed. As well as planting the surface of the compost (soil mix), it is also possible to make holes through the liner so that plants can be inserted around the sides. The most successful baskets are those in which the framework cannot be seen, as it is entirely masked by plants. In many cases, the hanging basket will look like a ball of plants.

A wide range of plants are available for baskets and an increasing number of trailing ones are being introduced. Many plants, such as pelargoniums and petunias, have trailing varieties as well as the more common bushy ones. Even snapdragons have been bred with a trailing habit. Any combination of plants can be used to create different schemes. A wonderful pot-pourri of colours can be achieved with a mixed planting, although a much more sophisticated effect can be created if you use plants in the same colour or even plants of just one variety. Baskets can be used individually or grouped together to produce a grander effect.

POPULAR ANNUALS FOR HANGING BASKETS

Anagallis	*Laurentia* (syn. *Isotoma*)
Antirrhinum (snapdragon)	*Lobelia*
Asarina	*Myosotis* (forget-me-not)
Begonia	*Nicotiana* (tobacco plant)
Bidens	*Pelargonium* (geranium)
Brachycome	*Petunia*
Camissonia	*Sanvitalia*
Cerinthe	*Schizanthus* (butterfly flower,
Chrysanthemum	poor man's orchid)
Diascia	*Senecio*
Echium	*Tagetes* (marigold)
Felicia	*Tropaeolum*
Fuchsia	(nasturtium)
Helichrysum	*Viola* × *wittrockiana* (pansy)

PLANTING A HANGING BASKET WITH ANNUALS

1 Assemble all the ingredients for making up the hanging basket, including compost (soil mix), water-retaining crystals and slow-release fertilizer.

2 Stand the basket on a large pot or bucket to make it easier to work with. Carefully place the liner in position so that it fills the basket.

3 Half fill the liner with compost (soil mix), then mix in some water-retaining crystals following the manufacturer's instructions to help prevent the basket drying out. Also add some slow-release fertilizer; this will remove the necessity to feed throughout the summer.

4 Cut holes about 4cm (1½in) across in the side of the liner. Shake some of the earth off the rootball of one of the side plants and wrap it in a strip of plastic. Poke it through the hole, remove the plastic and spread the roots out. When all the side plants are in place, fill up the basket with compost (soil mix), adding more water-retaining crystals and slow-release fertilizer.

5 Plant up the rest of the basket, packing the plants much more tightly together than you would in the open ground. Smooth out the surface of the compost (soil mix), removing any excess or adding a little more as necessary. Water, then hang the basket indoors until all danger of frost has passed.

Above: *The various types of pelargoniums are well suited to planting in a hanging basket. They make very cheerful planting partners. Here they are contrasted with verbena and trailing lobelia.*

PERENNIALS

The large gardens of past centuries, maintained by armies of gardeners, were never without the traditional herbaceous border, full of perennials of all kinds creating a veritable feast for the eyes. Today, even in the tiniest town garden or window box, we can draw on that tradition by growing the many old favourite varieties of perennials that are still widely available, and we can also take advantage of the enormous range of more recent introductions, many with improved qualities such as length of flowering time or resistance to pests and diseases. However you use them, whether you choose the traditional or modern varieties, perennials can form a structure for your garden scheme, providing a constant yet ever-changing source of pleasure throughout the seasons.

Left: *These chrysanthemums,* Dendranthema *'Belle' (red) and 'Honey' (yellow), create a stunning contrast.*

PERENNIALS DEFINED

What is a Perennial?

If we think about the most beautiful gardens we have seen, the feature they nearly all have in common is the colours of the perennial plants. There is, of course, a structural element, provided by trees and shrubs, but it is the perennials that give these gardens their vitality and, more often than not, their originality.

There are, literally, thousands of different perennial plants, offering gardeners a wide palette of colours, as well as a range of textures and shapes, to work with. This choice means that gardeners can create a unique that reflects their own tastes. While more experienced gardeners may include the ever-increasing number of varieties now available, less experienced gardeners can still create wonderful gardens, simply by using some of the reliable plants that have stood the test of time.

The expression "perennial plants" is rather imprecise. In theory it includes all plants that do not die after they have flowered. In practice, however, trees, shrubs, rock garden plants, and tropical and tender plants are usually excluded. Instead, perennials are usually regarded as plants that die back, either completely or partially, to ground level but that reappear the following year. They are sometimes also referred to as "herbaceous plants", but this term excludes those that do not completely die back, such as pinks (*Dianthus*), some irises and red-hot pokers (*Kniphofia*). Another term that is often used is "hardy perennials", which excludes those plants such as pelargoniums that are perennials only in warmer climates and have to be treated as annuals in colder areas.

Opposite: *Garden borders will reward the care and attention that you lavish on them.*

Above: *Canna leaves act as backdrop for the climber,* Rhodochiton atrosanguineus.

Above: *Lysimachia nummularia 'Aurea'*

Choosing a Scheme

One of the great advantages of using perennial plants in the garden is their versatility. The same basic selection of plants can be arranged in several ways to produce quite different results. In each situation, a plant will combine with its neighbours and take on the character of the scheme. Lady's mantle (*Alchemilla mollis*), for example, has a wonderfully old-fashioned look when combined with other such plants in a cottage garden. In a more formal arrangement, it can be used to provide an even block of yellowish-green, and, when it is grown near water, it takes on an entirely new character.

PERENNIAL USES

The versatility of perennials provides gardeners with the means to create whatever kind of garden appeals to them. Perennials can be planted in precise patterns, whereby symmetrical blocks of colour and shape are used to create a formal garden, while, at the other end of the spectrum, they can be allowed to run riot in the controlled chaos of a cottage garden. Between the two extremes is the herbaceous border, where the essential freedom of the cottage garden is married with the conscious arrangement of plants in the formal garden to create a bed that is very pleasing to the eye.

THE RIGHT PERENNIAL

Although perennial plants are versatile and, on the whole, forgiving, it is essential that when you plan your garden, whatever the proposed style, you

bear in mind the origins of the plants you wish to include. Plants always grow best in conditions that are similar to their natural habitat. An extreme example is pond plants, which are unlikely to grow in dry sand. In this case, the need to match the plant's location in the garden to its natural habitat will be obvious to most gardeners. However, many gardeners fail to consider the more subtle aspects of a plant's origins. For example, plants that naturally grow in full sun rarely do well in shady conditions, and nearly all the silver-leaved plants, which love the sun, will languish and die if planted in shade.

The design of your garden must, therefore, take into consideration the type of conditions that prevail in your local area. Most of the brightly coloured flowers appear on plants that grow in direct sun, for instance, whereas woodland

or shade planting relies on less colourful subjects and is more dependent on shapes, texture and the subtle colour variations of foliage.

While it is true that plants are best grown in conditions that are similar to those to which they are used in the wild, there is no reason why the conditions in your garden cannot be changed – to some extent, at least – to suit the plants you want to grow. For example, many plants like deep, rich soil, so it is hopeless trying to grow them on a light,

Above: *The fresh, bright colours of these stream-side plants make for a very attractive planting association. The jumbled colours create an informal effect.*

sandy soil. However, with effort, the conditions can be altered by adding plenty of well-rotted organic material, so that these plants can be grown.

The key to using perennials is to work with, rather than against, nature, because this is much more likely to produce satisfactory results.

Above: *Contrasting flowers and foliage produce an interesting picture. Here, the foaming flowers of lady's mantle* (Alchemilla mollis) *with the green, infertile fronds and the brown, fertile fronds of the royal fern* (Osmunda regalis) *create a perfect contrast, which is ideal for a formal or informal setting.*

Above right: *Try to blend the colours of foliage and flowers. Here, the silky, silver leaves of* Stachys byzantina *and the soft, bluish-purple flowers of* Nepeta × faassenii *combine to create a soft romantic image.*

Right: *This is a perfect example of the jumble of shapes, sizes and colours that produces the informality of the cottage garden.*

Cottage Gardens

Many people regard the traditional cottage garden as the epitome of beauty, a wonderful mixture of plants that seems to spill out in all directions. Indeed, such gardens often look as if the planting is out of control and the plants have been dotted here and there, seemingly at random. Cottage gardens may have looked like this a century ago, but today many gardeners are much more design-conscious in their approach and prefer to impose some form of discipline.

COTTAGE GARDEN STYLE

In the true cottage garden, plants were positioned where there was room, and there seemed to be no organization or overall design, with the resulting effect being a riot of plants and colour. The plants were situated close together, and any gaps were soon filled by self-seeded plants, again appearing at random. The tightness of the planting had the advantage of preventing weeds from surviving or even germinating, thus reducing the amount of work involved.

Modern cottage gardens, however, are rather more organized than the traditional ones. For example, species and varieties are kept together in clumps, rather than dotted about in a haphazard way. There is a tendency to ensure that the adjacent colours of the perennials blend with each other, rather than clash – we seem to be much more colour-conscious than our ancestors used to be. There is also more control in terms of the positioning of the plants, so that the smaller ones are at the front of the border and the taller ones are at the back.

That said, however, there is no reason why you should not let things run riot, if you so wish, and create a truly old-fashioned cottage garden.

OLD-FASHIONED PERENNIALS

One of the elements that gives the cottage garden its particular atmosphere is the use of "old-fashioned" plants, which may be described as plants that were grown by our ancestors and that are still grown today, largely unchanged. Apart from aesthetic reasons, there are other grounds for growing old-fashioned plants. The most important is that these plants have survived because they are tough. They are sufficiently resistant to the weather, pests and diseases to have lasted for several centuries. This means that many of them are relatively free of problems, making gardeners' lives easier.

Another reason for the enduring popularity of old-fashioned perennials is their appearance: they are, quite simply, attractive. They may not have the big, blowsy flowers in bold, bright colours that many modern plant breeders would have us like, but they are, nonetheless, usually covered in glorious flowers, often in subtle pastel shades, with occasional splashes of bright colour to liven up the border.

Modern plant breeding has concentrated so much on size and colour that scent has almost been bred out of many flowers. One advantage of the species and old varieties found in traditional cottage gardens is that they are often highly perfumed, an important quality in the make-up of a romantic cottage garden.

Left: *Spring in the cottage garden heralds the appearance of primulas, forget-me-nots, columbines and bluebells; all of these perennials are firm favourites with those who adopt this ever-popular style of gardening.*

Above: *A typical cottage garden path with plants spilling over it. The plants, such as the foxgloves (Digitalis purpurea) shown here, are allowed to self-seed where they like.*

Above: *The tight planting of a cottage garden allows little room for weeds to grow. Here, a mixture of self-sown annuals and planted perennials creates a wonderfully relaxed picture.*

Above: *Columbines (Aquilegia) contrast with the filmy foliage of fennel (Foeniculum vulgare).*

Above: *Greater masterwort (Astrantia major) has a lovely, old-fashioned quality that makes it a perfect subject for including in a cottage garden.*

COTTAGE GARDEN PERENNIALS

Alcea rosea (hollyhock)
Anemone × hybrida (Japanese anemone)
Aquilegia vulgaris (granny's bonnet)
Aster novae-angliae; *A. novi-belgii*
Astrantia major (masterwort)
Bellis perennis (double daisy)
Campanula persicifolia; *C. portenschlagiana;* *C. poscharskyana*
Centaurea cyanus (cornflower); *C. montana* (perennial cornflower)
Chrysanthemum
Delphinium
Dianthus (carnations, pinks)
Dicentra spectabilis (bleeding heart, Dutchman's trousers)
Doronicum (leopard's bane)
Galium odoratum, syn. *Asperula odorata* (woodruff)
Geranium ibericum
Geum rivale (water avens)
Lathyrus (vetchling)
Lupinus (lupin)
Lychnis chalcedonica (Jerusalem cross, Maltese cross)
Lysimachia nummularia (creeping Jenny)
Meconopsis cambrica (Welsh poppy)
Monarda didyma (bee balm, bergamot)
Myrrhis odorata (sweet cicely)
Paeonia officinalis (peony)
Polemonium caeruleum
Primula
Pulmonaria (lungwort)
Ranunculus aconitifolius (bachelor's buttons)
Saponaria officinalis (bouncing Bet)
Sedum spectabile (ice-plant)

Formal Gardens

As the name implies, formal gardens tend to be highly organized, with each plant in its place and no chance of self-sown seedlings appearing to disrupt the design. The overall plan is based on the use of symmetry, straight lines and smooth curves. It is this combination of regular lines and carefully positioned plants that makes the formal garden so different to the cottage garden, in which it can be said that anything goes.

FORMAL EFFECTS

A strictly formal garden is designed with precise regularity. The garden itself may be square or rectangular, but there should be a set piece in the centre, as well as borders around the edges. The planting on each side of the square or rectangular garden should be mirrored on the opposite side. Certain plants may also be repeated at intervals along the borders to create a sense of rhythm.

A formal garden may take the form of a parterre, in which the borders are contained by low hedging. This may be provided by a shrubby plant, such as box (*Buxus*), or by plants like santolina or germander (*Teucrium*), which are technically shrubs or sub-shrubs, but usually regarded as perennials in the garden. Within the hedges, perennials of a uniform colour and size are set out in blocks, or a variety of plants are laid out in a pattern that is then echoed elsewhere in the design.

Not all formal gardens are symmetrical. Some schemes that may be considered formal have no real formality at all, depending more on simplicity for the effect they produce. In this type of garden the number of plants is severely restricted. There might be, for example, one or two well-chosen plants, sited in telling positions. Alternatively, there may be a formal pond, with plants in one corner – a tall reed, perhaps, or three plants, a taller one with two others in front, forming a close triangle. Other arrangements might include a single clump of tall grass or bamboo in a gravelled area.

Plants in a formal garden often play a lesser role than features such as hedges, paths, statuary, large ponds and fountains. When plants are introduced, they are often selected for their architectural qualities – a single clump of flax lily (*Phormium*), for example. A cabbage tree (*Cordyline*), with its even spread of pointed leaves, is another perfect plant for such a garden, whether planted directly in the ground or grown in a container.

Stark formality is not really the business of this book. We are more concerned with the use of perennials, and formal gardens, attractive though they often are, do not use as many different perennials as most gardeners would like. However, if you feel that a formal garden is the right choice for you, remember that there are many occasions when perennials can be organized in a formal way, while many of the plants that are suggested for less formal gardens can also be used to create an eye-catching, symmetrical scheme.

Above: *Grasses have simple, elegant shapes that rarely look fussy. This makes them suitable for formal settings, either used as single specimens or planted in groups, as is the case here.*

Above: *Foliage is often more important than flowers in a formal setting, as is demonstrated by this group that is dominated by* Euphorbia mellifera. *The coolness of the greens looks very striking in combination with the white stone planter.*

Above right: *Rhythm and repetition in a garden create a feeling of formality, as does the use of straight lines and simple shapes. The clipped box balls in this formal garden contribute to the overall effect by creating a satisfying rhythm down the length of the garden.*

Right: *This large sunken garden shows how a formal layout can be softened with well-placed plants such as lady's mantle (*Alchemilla mollis*), whose foaming, lime-green flowers are spilling out over the edges of the paths.*

Herbaceous Borders

A herbaceous border is simply a border devoted to herbaceous plants. At the end of the year all the plants die back, but then sprout anew the following spring. A large herbaceous border in full flower is a wonderful sight and more than compensates for the empty winter months when there are fewer perennials to see.

THE SIZE OF THE BORDER

In the past, herbaceous borders tended to be extensive and required the attention of a large number of gardeners. However, a successful herbaceous border need be neither large nor labour-intensive. It is perfectly true that a huge herbaceous border several hundred metres (yards) long is an incredible sight, but then so is one that extends for only about ten metres or less. Unlike the Victorians, we do not necessarily believe that the size of a border is a measure of its effectiveness. We are probably more concerned with the plants that are growing there.

When it comes to the amount of labour needed to maintain herbaceous borders, it is a mistake to think that you need a staff of full-time gardeners to ensure that they look their best. You will definitely need help if your borders are several hundred metres long, but the borders that can be accommodated in most of today's private gardens can be looked after by the owner. As long as the ground is well prepared in the first place and work is carried out early in the year, before the weeds can get a hold, herbaceous borders are easy and, in fact, pleasurable to maintain.

SEASONAL CHANGES

The winter months can be a problem for those who feel that the garden must offer something all year round. In the old days herbaceous borders were often part of a larger garden, in which there were plenty of other areas to see during the winter months, including, in the very largest gardens, tropical glasshouses!

Today, however, many gardeners are as interested in the dried remains of the perennials as they are in their appearance when in full growth. Many plants die very gracefully, and their bare, dead stems can be unexpectedly attractive. Grasses, in particular, are useful in this respect, but there are many other plants, either in clumps or as individual stems, that are eye-catching in dull, winter light. These remains also, of course, provide invaluable food and shelter for birds and insects.

CHOOSING THE COLOURS

The design of a herbaceous border is a matter of personal preference, and individual tastes can all be accommodated using the incredible range of plants now available. The perennials are usually grouped so that the colours blend harmoniously. They are often arranged so that the hotter colours are in the centre and the cooler tones at the ends of the border. It is also possible to create borders that are restricted to only one colour or to a group of colours – pastel shades or hot colours, for example. Some gardeners prefer a white border or one that is limited to plants that have yellow and blue flowers and foliage. The number of variations on these themes is almost limitless, and each offers the possibility of a border that is unique.

Below: *This is a typical layout, with twin herbaceous borders separated by a wide path. Such a planting scheme is unbeatable in midsummer.*

Above: *An informal herbaceous border that relies on both foliage and flowers for its effect, contrasting grasses and hostas with Welsh poppies* (Meconopsis cambrica) *and columbines* (Aquilegia).

Above: *A vivid contrast between the purple of this* Phlox *and the silver foliage of the* Anaphalis *brings alive this section of the border. Too much contrast, however, would create an uncomfortable effect.*

Above: *A daylily (*Hemerocallis*) peeping through the delicate, silver foliage of an* Artemisia *makes for a wonderful contrast of flower and foliage.*

Right: *Dedicated colour schemes can produce particularly striking results. Here, a gravel-edged border has been filled with perennials in a range of hot colours, creating a bright, cheerful atmosphere.*

Mixed Borders

An increase in interest in the mixed border came with the decline in popularity of the herbaceous border earlier this century. The mixed border is so-called because, of course, it contains a mixture of plants. It is not restricted solely to herbaceous plants, but can also include shrubs and even trees.

THE ADVANTAGES

Devotees prefer the mixed border to the traditional herbaceous border for several reasons. The main reason is that including trees and shrubs gives the border a clear structure and a permanent framework. Even in winter there is something to see, especially if the shrubs are evergreen. Although many herbaceous plants have a relatively long season of interest, many have only a brief one. This can be regarded as an advantage in many ways – borders that are dynamic and ever-changing make for a much more interesting garden. The sudden blooming of a clump of red flowers, for example, not only provides a point of interest, but also changes the whole appearance of the border. The advantages of a mixed border are easier to understand if you contrast this type of border with, say, an annual bedding scheme, which remains largely the same throughout the summer and autumn.

COMBINING THE PLANTS

Some gardeners do not like too much change in the garden but prefer to have one or two anchor points that provide a permanent structure within which the perennials can be allowed to weave their constantly changing thread. In some respects, reducing the amount of change in a border emphasizes what remains.

Including trees and shrubs widens the scope of plants that can be used in a border and introduces a wider variety of shapes and textures into the overall design. In general, trees and shrubs also have a more "solid" appearance, which is important, whether they are dotted around the border, grouped together or even used as a backdrop. This structure is particularly important if there is no proper background to the border, such as a hedge or wall.

Many perennials often look their best when grown with shrubs. A clump of day lilies (*Hemerocallis*), for example, peeping out from between two shrubs, can look superb.

Another advantage of incorporating trees and shrubs into a border is that they provide shade. Although many gardeners try to avoid shade, it does provide a habitat for a wider range of perennials than could otherwise be grown in a border.

Left: *Most cottage gardens are a delightful mixture of annuals, perennials, shrubs and climbers. A cottage garden made up of borders with a well-chosen mixture of annuals and perennials will give you a long-lasting display of flowers, with ever-changing points of interest.*

Above: *Annuals, perennials and shrubs all play a part in this tightly packed planting scheme. The colours, textures and shapes of the plants are used to good effect to create an eye-catching border.*

Above: *Combining perennials with shrubs – here* Sisyrinchium striatum *is growing with* Rosa *'Félicité Perpétue' – allows for a greater variety of planting and hence a more interesting scheme than could be achieved using perennials alone.*

Right: *Some shrubs are regarded as "honorary" perennials. Herbs, such as the sage shown here, as well as lavender and rosemary, are frequently seen in association with perennials.*

Island Beds

Although they have long been a part of the bedding plant tradition, it is only relatively recently that island beds have become an acknowledged element of the perennial scene. Island beds are simply borders that you can walk around completely, and so view from all angles. They may be positioned in the centre of a lawn or within a paved area, or they can be circumnavigated by a path.

SHAPES AND SIZES
The shapes of island beds can vary enormously. In more formal gardens, the shapes should be regular, including circles, ovals and squares. However, triangles should be avoided, unless they are large, because it is difficult to plant the corners of a triangle satisfactorily, especially if they come to a sharp point.

Formal shapes do not, however, lend themselves particularly well to the informality of most perennial plants, for which larger, free-form beds are usually much more satisfactory. By this is meant a self-contained bed that has a sinuous edge. The line of the edge should not be determined at random, however, since it always looks better if it reflects the shape of a nearby border or path, or swings out around a tree or some other garden feature.

Allied to the shape is the size of the bed: a simple rule to remember is that perennial island beds should never be too small. In fact, if the shape of the bed can be taken in at a glance, the bed is probably too small. The best island beds are large enough to accommodate some tall plants, or even some trees and shrubs in the centre of the bed in order to introduce some height. The worst beds are those in which there is not enough space for the plants to develop any height. In such beds, your eyes are likely to sweep straight across the planting to whatever lies beyond.

CHOOSING THE PERENNIALS
The idea of looking beyond the bed is an important one. When you are planning both the size and contents of the bed, always make sure that it is filled with plants of an appropriate height and density. No plant looks its best if you can see straight though it. A thin scattering of low plants usually looks unappealing and does little for the overall appearance of the garden.

One of the advantages of an island bed is that it can be sited in the open, away from the shade, with plenty of air circulating among the plants. This type of position is greatly appreciated by many sun-loving plants. In larger island beds, however, where there is a central planting of small trees and shrubs, shade will be created on one side. The shade will vary in intensity across the bed and provide an opportunity to grow a range of plants that have different growing requirements.

CREATING A CIRCULAR BED

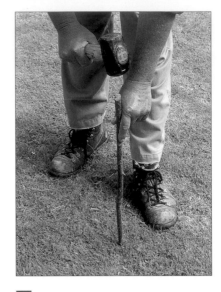

1 Insert a post in the centre of the proposed bed. Attach one end of a piece of string to the post and the other end to a bottle filled with sand or peat.

2 Walk slowly around the post, keeping the string taut and the bottle tilted, so that the sand trickles out and marks the outline of the circle.

CREATING AN IRREGULAR BED

Use a flexible hosepipe to work out the size and shape of an irregular bed. Once you are happy with the shape of the bed, remove a line of turf around the edge of the pipe to mark it out.

3 Once the circle is complete, the turf can be cut from within the marked area in order to produce a perfectly circular bed.

CREATING AN OVAL BED

Place two posts in the ground and loosely tie a piece of string around them. Experiment with the distance between the posts and the length of the piece of string to get the size and shape of bed you require. Place a bottle filled with peat or sand inside the loop of string and walk around the posts, keeping the string taut. The sand trickles out of the bottle, creating the outline of a perfect oval.

PREPARING THE GROUND

1 With many lawn grasses, it will not be necessary to use a herbicide; simply skim off the surface grass and dig out any roots that remain.

2 Dig the soil, removing any weeds and stones. Mix in plenty of organic material as you dig to encourage the roots to grow deeply.

3 Leave the bed to weather for a few months after digging, and remove any residual weeds. Fork in well-rotted compost and rake level before planting.

Above: *This island bed is filled with an array of colourful perennials and surrounded by mown grass paths.*

Shady Plantings

Many gardeners regard areas of shade as a problem, but they can be an advantage in many ways, because they provide a greater variety of habitats, thus increasing the range of plants that can be grown. Shade is not something to worry about, as so many gardeners seem to do.

SUITABLE PERENNIALS

The golden rule when planting shady areas is to use perennials that grow naturally in the shade. If this rule is followed, you should have no difficulty in establishing a fine range of perennials. It may seem an obvious point to make, but the main reason so many gardeners dread gardening in shady areas is because they want to grow the brightly coloured plants that thrive in full sun. They plant them in shady borders, and they quickly become drawn and etiolated, as they struggle to the light; then they turn sickly because they are undernourished and short of light. This, in turn, means that they are more susceptible to disease, and, before long, the plants die. If you choose plants that like the shade, the results will be completely different.

DEGREES OF SHADE

It is important to distinguish between the different types of shade and to give your perennials the right conditions. The first kind of shade is known as light or partial shade. This includes areas that are in sun for part of the day or are lightly shaded by objects through which the sun can penetrate from time to time. The mottled light under some trees comes into this category, which also includes areas such as the north side of a building where the sun does not reach, but where there is always light from above.

Dense shade is defined as an area in which sunlight never penetrates and the low levels of light make the site gloomy. This type of shade is much more problematic. Fortunately, few gardens are entirely in dense shade, although there may be one or two small areas that are.

You can alter the level of shade in parts of the garden. If you have a large tree, for example, removing the lower branches allows more light to reach the ground beneath. The branches in the main canopy can also be thinned to create a dappled light. In a dark, north-facing area, a fence or wall opposite the site can be painted white to reflect the available light towards the shady bed.

Above: *Many hellebores, including this* Helleborus odorus, *grow well in light shade.*

Left: Geranium macrorrhizum *is one of the best perennial plants for growing in shade. Here, it is flowering well in fairly dark conditions.*

Some shade-loving perennials, such as pulmonarias and hellebores, can be planted under deciduous trees, which have lost their leaves during the perennials' main flowering season, thus providing plenty of light at the crucial time when these plants produce their flowers.

Remember, too, that the type of soil is important. Many shade-loving perennials are naturally woodland plants, and so need a woodland-like soil. This should be high in organic materials, such as leafmould, which hold plenty of moisture. Some perennials will grow in dry woodland soils – *Euphorbia amygdaloides robbiae*, for example – but for a greater range of plants it is better to modify the soil in order to create better conditions.

Above: *Both primulas and ferns relish growing in light shade. Plants always do well if given the conditions they prefer.*

Above: *Columbines are usually grown in the open border, but are frequently found in open woodland in the wild. Why not follow nature and use them in shady borders?*

SHADE-LOVING PERENNIALS

Achlys triphylla
Actaea alba (white baneberry); *A. rubra* (red baneberry)
Alchemilla mollis (lady's mantle)
Anemone nemorosa (wood anemone)
Aruncus dioicus (goat's beard)
Asarum caudatum; *A. hartwegii*
Begonia grandis evansiana (hardy begonia)
Bergenia (elephant's ears)
Brunnera macrophylla, syn. *Anchusa myosotidiflora*
Caltha palustris (kingcup, marsh marigold)
Campanula latifolia
Cardamine bulbifera; *C. enneaphyllos*; *C. kitaibelii*; *C. pentaphyllos*
Carex pendula (pendulous sedge)
Convallaria majalis (lily-of-the-valley)
Corydalis flexuosa
Dicentra
Disporum (fairy bells)
Dryopteris filix-mas (male fern)
Epimedium
Eranthis hyemalis (winter aconite)
Euphorbia amygdaloides (wood spurge); *E. amygdaloides robbiae*
Geranium (cranesbill; some)
Glaucidium palmatum
Hacquetia epipactis
Helleborus (hellebore)
Hosta
Houttuynia cordata
Iris foetidissima (stinking iris)
Jeffersonia diphylla; *J. dubia*
Kirengeshoma palmata
Lamium galeobdolon (yellow archangel)

Lathyrus vernus (spring vetchling)
Lilium martagon (Turk's cap lily)
Liriope muscari (lilyturf)
Meconopsis (blue poppy)
Milium effusum 'Aureum' (Bowles' golden grass)
Myosotis sylvatica (garden forget-me-not)
Omphalodes cappadocica; *O. verna* (blue-eyed Mary)
Oxalis acetosella (wood sorrel)
Paris (herb Paris)
Pentaglottis sempervirens
Persicaria affinis (syn. *Polygonum affine*)
Phlox divaricata (blue phlox, wild sweet William); *P. stolonifera* (creeping phlox)
Podophyllum hexandrum (syn. *P. emodi*), *P. peltatum* (May apple)
Polygonatum (Solomon's seal)
Polystichum setiferum (soft shield fern)
Primula
Pulmonaria (lungwort)
Sanguinaria canadensis (bloodroot)
Smilacina racemosa (false spikenard); *S. stellata* (star flower)
Smyrnium perfoliatum
Stylophorum
Symphytum ibericum (syn. *S. grandiflorum*)
Tellima grandiflora
Tiarella (foamflower)
Trillium (wood lily)
Uvularia (merrybells)
Vancouveria
Viola odorata (sweet violet); *V. riviniana* Purpurea Group (Labrador violet)
Waldsteinia ternata

Waterside Plantings

Water is an invaluable addition to any garden, partly because it allows a whole new range of plants and wildlife to flourish. Water in the garden also has a very soothing effect. The sound of water tinkling from a fountain or running in a stream is utterly relaxing. Watching the constantly moving reflections of sunlight, sky and the surrounding vegetation can also be wonderfully calming and almost hypnotic.

THE BENEFITS OF WATER

Water attracts wildlife, and a pond will encourage birds as well as beautiful insects, such as dragonflies and damselflies, to visit the garden. The shape of the pond is important – where a natural pond is appropriate for a wildlife garden, a pond with a rigid concrete surround is more suitable for a more formal garden.

For the gardener who is interested in perennial plants, however, the main attraction of a pond is the range of plants that it is possible to grow. A pond provides three areas for planting that are not available in a garden without water. The first area is in the water itself, which will enable you to grow a wide variety of plants such as waterlilies (*Nymphaea*). These can be planted in the mud at the bottom of a naturally occurring pond, but if your pond is lined they will have to be planted in special baskets.

The next planting is the shallow water at the edge of the pond. The plants suitable for these conditions include the beautiful *Iris laevigata* and its cultivars, which, again, can be grown in the mud or in baskets. When you are constructing a pond, it is important to create a series of tiers around the edge. This provides different planting depths, so that you can include a variety of plants, as some water plants prefer shallower conditions than others.

Finally, there are the damp margins of the pond. Many plants thrive on the shore, rather than in the water, although several of the plants that grow in shallow water will also survive in the conditions at the margins of the pond because they are used to water rising and falling in their natural habitats.

If you are building a pond with a liner, it is always a good idea to run the liner under the soil some way from the margin of the pond in order to create a damp patch. If the liner comes up to the surface right at the edge of the pond, then the soil on the bank will be too dry to grow pond plants.

Even if you do not have a pond, it is possible to create a boggy area by digging a depression, lining it with a sheet of pond liner, and filling it with a rich mixture of good soil and organic matter. Puncture a few drainage holes in the liner so that stagnant water does not accumulate. Such an area will be a lush haven of plants, even in very dry weather.

Above: *Some plants, such as these waterlilies (*Nymphaea*), will only grow in water where the leaves and flowers can float. They cannot be grown in ordinary soil or even a bog garden.*

Left: *These rodgersias are typical of many plants that like waterside conditions. They are lush, healthy, and growing well.*

WATERSIDE PERENNIALS

Aruncus (goat's beard)
Astilbe
Caltha
Cardamine (bitter cress)
Cimicifuga (bugbane)
Darmera peltata,
 syn. *Peltiphyllum peltatum*
 (umbrella plant)
Eupatorium
Filipendula
 (meadowsweet)
Gunnera
Hosta
Iris ensata, syn. *I. kaempferi*
 (Japanese water iris);
 I. sibirica
Ligularia (leopard plant)
Lobelia cardinalis
 (cardinal flower)

Lysichiton (bog arum,
 skunk cabbage)
Lysimachia (yellow loosestrife)
Lythrum (purple loosestrife)
Mimulus (monkey flower,
 musk)
Onoclea sensibilis
 (sensitive fern)
Osmunda regalis (royal fern)
Persicaria bistorta, syn.
 Polygonum bistorta
 (bistort, snakeweed)
Phragmites
Primula
Rheum (ornamental rhubarb)
Rodgersia
Trollius (globeflower)
Zantedeschia aethiopica
 (arum lily)

Above: *Waterlilies (*Nymphaea*) often form a vast raft of foliage. Like many other garden plants, there are times when they need to be kept in check.*

Above: *The arum lily,* Zantedeschia aethiopica, *is perfect for a waterside planting. It will also grow in shallow water.*

Above: *A good waterside planting in which the ebullience of the yellow mimulus contrasts well with the restrained foliage of the hosta.*

Wild Flower Plantings

In some respects all flower gardens may be described as wild flower plantings. Every plant we grow in our gardens, including the species, which are undoubtedly wild flowers, as well as the other highly bred forms that we can buy today, originated somewhere in the wild. However, the term "wild flowers" is usually taken to mean those flowers that grow wild in the local area.

WILD FLOWER HABITATS

Increasing pressure on the countryside means that the number of wild flowers is diminishing, and, unfortunately, this is a worldwide problem. One way of combating this demise is by creating wild flower habitats within our own gardens. Such areas, in turn, have the benefit of reintroducing wildlife, especially in the form of insects, such as butterflies, which thrive on the native plants, but are less happy on many of the introduced or hybridized ones that we grow in our gardens. On the whole, most wild flowers are not as attractive individually as cultivated ones, but when they are gathered together in, say, a meadow garden, their beauty becomes much more apparent.

WILD FLOWER GARDENS

One might expect growing wild plants to be fairly easy, but establishing and maintaining a wild flower garden is one of the most difficult types of gardening. There is the natural tendency, especially in cultivated ground, for the ranker weeds to take over and smother the plants you want to encourage. Success depends largely on the way you approach the task as well as on the initial preparation.

The first method is to allow wild flowers to colonize some existing grass. If this is a lawn, you should not have many problems, but if you are lucky enough to have a field, the grasses are likely to be too rank for the flowers to survive. The first task is to spend a year mowing the grass at regular intervals to keep it short. This will kill off most of the ranker grasses and leave the finer ones.

The next step, whether you have a field or a lawn, is to put in wild flower plants at random throughout the meadow. You can scatter the seed directly over the area, if you wish, but the competition is intense, and so it is better to sow the seed in trays, prick out and grow on the plants in pots first. Plant out in spring when the perennials are strong enough to compete. Once established, they will self-sow, which is always more successful than simply scattering the seed.

The second method is to clear the ground completely, removing all traces of perennial weeds. Then, sow a wild flower and grass seed mixture that has been especially formulated for your area. There are several suppliers for this type of seed. It is worth finding the right seed mixture, as it is important to use only those perennials that already grow, or are likely to grow, in your area. These will have the best chance of surviving. For example, there is little point in trying to naturalize plants from chalk (alkaline) downland on acid heathland soil.

Once the meadow is established, it should be cut regularly, about once or twice a year, to prevent the rank weeds from taking over. The best time is usually in summer once the main flush of plants have seeded.

Above: *Here, wild flowers are growing to great effect in a herbaceous border. Evening primrose* (Oenothera biennis) *and feverfew* (Tanacetum parthenium) *make a sympathetic planting combination.*

On a much smaller scale it is also possible to create a wild flower garden simply by sowing or planting perennials along a hedgerow, which is another natural habitat in itself.

PERENNIALS FOR WILD FLOWER PLANTINGS

Achillea millefolium
(milfoil)
Ajuga reptans
(common bugle)
Asclepias tuberosa
(butterfly weed)
*Campanula
rotundifolia* (harebell)
Cardamine pratensis
(cuckoo flower,
lady's smock)
Centaurea scabiosa
Fritillaria meleagris
(snake's head fritillary;
this is a bulb)
Geranium pratense
(meadow cranesbill)
Hypericum perforatum
(St. John's wort)

Leontodon hispidus
(rough hawkbit)
Malva moschata
(musk mallow)
Monarda fistulosa
(wild bergamot)
Narcissus pseudonarcissus
(Lent Lily; this is a bulb)
Primula veris (cowslip)
Prunella vulgaris
Ranunculus acris
(meadow buttercup);
R. bulbosus (bulbous
buttercup); *R. repens*
(creeping buttercup)
Stellaria graminea
(lesser stitchwort)
Succisa pratensis
(devil's bit scabious)

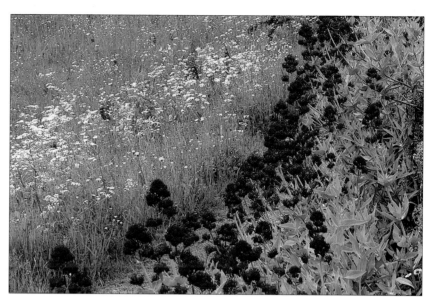

Above: *A beautiful wild flower meadow edged with red valerian* (Centranthus ruber*) that is growing in an old wall.*

Above: *Many garden flowers are forms of wild flowers.* Ajuga reptans *'Catlin's Giant' is a large form of the species.*

Above: *Wild flowers can also be planted in shade.* Anemone nemorosa *and* Ranunculus auricomis *are both woodlanders.*

Container Plantings

There is a tendency to think of perennials in terms of the herbaceous border or bed, and, while it is true that they are border plants par excellence, many can also be used as container plants. As with most of the ways in which you can use perennials, the possibilities are endless, with new ideas for container plantings appearing all the time.

PERENNIALS FOR CONTAINERS

Many of the so-called "annuals" that are used in windowboxes and hanging baskets are, in fact, perennials, but most, such as pelargoniums and petunias, are tender, and are therefore treated as annuals. Others are on the borderline of hardiness and may survive mild winters, but it is the true hardy perennials that we are considering here.

On the whole, it is much more effective to plant perennials in a container as individual species or varieties, rather than using them in mixed plantings. This is partly because they look best like this, but it also has a lot to do with the size of the plants – if you have a large flax lily (*Phormium*) in a pot, there is not much room for anything else.

When plants are grown in isolation in this way, it is also much easier to appreciate them than when they are part of a busy border. For example, the fountain-like foliage of a hosta in a pot will stand out against stone or brick paving in a way that would be impossible if the same plant were surrounded by other foliage. Similarly, the spiky appearance of a cabbage tree (*Cordyline*) can also be fully appreciated in a container on a plinth, silhouetted against a plain background or the sky.

Perennials in containers can be used in a variety of ways. Placing the container in a border may seem rather odd, but this can be a good way of filling any gaps – a pot of African lilies (*Agapanthus*), for example, can be stood in the gap left when a spring-flowering plant dies back.

When they are raised on plinths, containers also work well as focal points. For example, a large container on a plinth might be placed in a border, positioned at the end of a path, or at the edge or centre of the lawn. The eye is drawn immediately to the container, and this is the perfect way to focus a visitor's attention towards – or even away from – another garden feature. Containers can also be used to great advantage in more obvious places, notably on patios, either arranged in groups or used singly to show off individual specimens.

The other great advantage of container-grown perennials is that they can be moved around to create fresh displays, and, as the flowers of one plant go over, another coming into bloom can be moved in to replace it, producing an ever-changing scene in the border.

Containers are also the ideal way of decorating or drawing attention to a flight of stairs. They can be positioned on the highest or lowest steps to guide the eye up or down. They can also be set to stand guard on each side of a doorway or arch, thus creating a well-defined entrance to the house or garden.

Left: *The beautiful mauve flowers of* Convolvulus sabatius *complement the warm, terracotta colour of the pot. Being a slightly tender plant, the convolvulus can be moved inside in its pot for the winter.*

PLANTING A CONTAINER

1 These are the materials you will need to plant a container. They include a terracotta pot, your choice of plant (in this case, a cordyline), some stones for drainage, potting compost (soil mix), slow-release fertilizer (either loose or in pellets) and water-retaining granules.

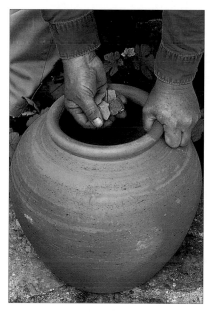

2 Cover the bottom of the container with small stones or some pieces of tile or pottery, so that water can drain freely from the pot.

3 Partly fill the pot with a good quality potting compost. Some loose slow-release fertilizer and water-retaining granules can be mixed with the compost before filling the pot.

4 Scoop a hole in the compost and insert the plant, positioning it so that the top of the rootball will be level with the surface of the compost.

5 Place any extra plants you wish to include around the edge of the main plant. Add more compost to fill any gaps, and firm down.

6 Insert a fertilizer pellet if you have decided to use one, rather than the loose fertilizer granules. Water thoroughly.

7 The plants will soon grow away and fill out the container.

Fragrant Perennials

As you would expect from a range of plants as diverse as the perennials, there are a number that are fragrant, which adds to the enjoyment of growing them.

THE SCENTED GARDEN

It is possible to create borders especially devoted to scent, but, in many ways, it is more exciting to come across a fragrance at random. If too many fragrant plants are placed together, the various fragrances may conflict with each other, so they can be appreciated neither singly nor together. Placing scented plants judiciously around the garden, on the other hand, means that individual scents can suddenly assail you as you walk around, often before you are conscious of the plants themselves.

Although it is pleasant to come across scents as you walk along a border, it is often far more enjoyable to relax on a seat or in an arbour that has perfumed plants set near to it. This is a particularly good idea if you have a patio where you can eat on a summer's evening. Many plants are evening-scented, and sitting in the garden after a hard day's work, as the light begins to fade and the scents start to float on the warm air, is one of the most pleasant and effective ways to relax and forget the problems of the day.

A similar idea is to position scented plants near doors and windows that are likely to be open, so that the scents waft in and fill the room. Planting your favourite scented plant near to the drive so that it welcomes you as you arrive home is also a sure way to emphasize the break between work and home.

CAPTURING THE SCENT

Scent can be elusive. Sometimes it travels a long way on the air and at other times you have to place your nose in the flower before it becomes apparent. Some scents have to react with the air before they can be smelt – when you are close to the flower you cannot smell anything, but move a few feet away, and there it is.

Other scents are not given off until the plant is bruised. *Artemisia*, for example, does not smell until you gently crush its leaves. Plants of this type should be planted close to paths, so that their scent is released as you brush past them. Catmint or catnip (*Nepeta cataria*) is good for this.

You should remember that not all plants are pleasantly fragrant. Your family will not be appreciative if you plant a dragon arum (*Dracunculus vulgaris*) under a window. It is a striking plant, but put it at the bottom of the garden because it has a strong foetid smell, rather like rotten flesh, which it uses to attract flies.

Remember, too, that not everyone likes the same scents – *Phuopsis stylosa*, for example, has a foxy, rather pungent smell that some people dislike. Some scents change in character during the day – for instance, *Cestrum parqui* has a strong savoury smell during the day, but a sweet fragrance at night.

Above all, remember that while much pleasure can be obtained from scented plants, they must always be used with discretion.

Left: *Lupins have a very distinctive, peppery scent, which, like many plant perfumes, is most apparent in warm weather.*

SCENTED FLOWERS

Acorus calamus (sweet flag)
Adenophora liliifolia
Aponogeton distachyos
 (water hawthorn)
Asphodeline lutea
 (syn. *Asphodelus luteus*)
Calanthe discolor
Cestrum parqui
Chrysanthemum
Clematis heracleifolia;
 C. recta
Convallaria majalis
 (lily-of-the-valley)
Cosmos atrosanguineus
 (chocolate cosmos)
Crambe cordifolia;
 C. maritima (seakale)
Delphinium wellbyi
 (syn. *D. leroyi*)
Dianthus (carnations, pinks)
Filipendula ulmaria
Helleborus lividus
Hemerocallis citrina;
 H. dumortieri;
 H. lilioasphodelus (syn.
 H. flava); *H. middendorffii;*
 H. multiflora
Hosta 'Honeybells';
 H. plantaginea
Iris 'Florentina';
 I. germanica (common
 German flag); *I. hoogiana;*
 I. pallida dalmatica;

I. unguicularis (Algerian iris)
Lobularia maritima,
 syn. *Alyssum maritimum*
 (sweet alyssum)
Lunaria rediviva
 (perennial honesty)
Lupinus polyphyllus
Mirabilis jalapa
 (four o'clock flower)
Paeonia (peony; some)
Petasites fragrans (winter
 heliotrope); *P. japonicus*
 giganteus
Phlox maculata (meadow
 phlox; wild sweet William);
 P. paniculata (perennial
 phlox)
Polygonatum × *hybridum*
 (syn. *P. multiflorum*)
Primula alpicola; *P. florindae*
 (giant cowslip); *P. secundiflora*;
 P. sikkimensis (Himalayan
 cowslip)
Romneya coulteri
 (Californian poppy);
 R. coulteri trichocalyx
Smilacina racemosa (false
 spikenard)
Tellima grandiflora
Verbena bonariensis
 (purple top); *V. corymbosa*
Yucca filamentosa (Adam's
 needle)

SCENTED FOLIAGE

Agastache foeniculum (syn.
 A. anethiodora, A anisata);
 A. mexicana (Mexican
 giant hyssop)
Anthemis punctata
 cupaniana
Artemisia (wormwood)
Melittis melissophyllum
Meum athamanticum
 (spignel)
Nepeta (catmint)
Salvia (sage)

Above: *Not all flowers can be smelt from a distance. You need to be quite close to irises to catch their fragrance.*

Above: *The lily-of-the-valley* (Convallaria majalis) *is one of the best loved of all scented cottage garden plants.*

Left: *Old-fashioned cottage garden plants, such as this lupin, are more likely to have perfumed flowers than many of the modern hybrids.*

Above: *Old-fashioned pinks* (Dianthus) *have a wonderful scent, but a short flowering season. A few of the modern hybrids are also scented, but flower for longer.*

Climbing Perennials

When we think of climbing plants, it is usually the shrubby types that come to mind: roses, clematis, honeysuckles and many other cottage garden favourites. However, there are also a number of perennial climbers, some of which can be a wonderfully colourful addition to the garden.

CLIMBERS FOR SHRUBS

One of the most important points to remember about climbers is that they need something to climb up. In the wild, they usually climb up other plants such as trees or shrubs. In the garden, this is not only a possibility, but also a good idea. This is because many shrubs are at their best when they are in flower and, if this happens to be in the spring, then they are dependent on their foliage to provide interest for the rest of the year. So, one way to brighten up a shrub is to grow another plant through it that produces flowers later in the season. Flame creeper (*Tropaeolum speciosum*) is ideal for this, and will happily grow over low shrubs, producing masses of flame-red flowers.

A similar idea is to grow a climbing perennial through another more vigorous climber – the Chilean glory flower (*Eccremocarpus scaber*), for example, will grow through an early-flowering clematis and produce its flowers in late summer and early autumn. Hedges can also be used as supports, as long as the plant is robust enough to stand the competition. Greater periwinkle (*Vinca major*) is ideal for using in this way, and looks superb in spring when its blue flowers peep out from what might otherwise be a dull hedge.

Providing an artificial framework is another way to grow perennial climbers. This is best done in the perennial border by erecting wooden structures such as pyramids, tripods or even simple poles. These provide robust supports which the plants can climb up, or, if they are not self-clinging, against which they can be tied. Most perennial climbers do not grow very high, so the supporting structures do not have to be very tall, and wicker is the perfect material in this instance. Similarly, *Clematis recta*, like many other perennial plants, only needs the help of some peasticks or metal plant supports in order to form a pleasingly rounded shape.

Some perennial climbers are quite vigorous and are suitable for growing over arches or trellises. The golden hop (*Humulus lupulus* 'Aureus') is a perfect example of such a plant. It can also be trained over a framework to make a secluded arbour. However, the stems are rough and can cause serious weals if they rub against the skin, so it is important to make sure that you tie in all the straggling stems.

As a last resort, one way of using perennial climbers, especially if they are not too vigorous, is to leave them alone and allow them to scramble over the ground, forming a loose, straggling pile. Some clematis, such as *Clematis heracleifolia*, are particularly good for this.

Below: *Many perennials, such as these violas and armerias, will scramble quite happily through low shrubs, using them as supports in order to get closer to the light.*

PERENNIAL CLIMBERS AND SCRAMBLERS

Clematis × eriostemon;
C. × durandii;
C. heracleifolia;
C. × jouiniana; C. recta
Codonopsis (bonnet
bellflower)
Eccremocarpus scaber
(Chilean glory flower)
Humulus lupulus 'Aureus'
(golden hop)

Lathyrus sylvestris (perennial
pea)
Rhodochiton atrosanguineus
(purple bells)
Solanum dulcamara
'Variegatum' (poisonous)
Tropaeolum speciosum
(flame creeper); *T. tuberosum*
Vinca major (greater
periwinkle)

Above: Clematis recta *is an
excellent herbaceous clematis. It
can either grow through a low
shrub or brushwood supports, or
simply be left to form a mound.*

Right: *The golden hop,* Humulus
lupulus *'Aureus', puts on a
tremendous amount of growth
each year, although it takes a few
years to reach its full potential.*

Perennials for Ground Cover

Plants that act as ground cover do just that – they cover the ground. For the gardener, there are both horticultural and visual advantages to this. From the horticultural point of view, a plant that covers the ground thoroughly should be welcomed because it will, in theory, help to reduce the number of weeds in the beds and borders. This works on the principle that the plant is so dense that little light can reach the ground and any weed seedlings that do manage to germinate are starved of light, become drawn and sickly, and soon die.

HORTICULTURAL ADVANTAGES

Ground cover is not quite the answer to every gardener's dreams as is sometimes implied. Simply excluding light does not necessarily guarantee that there will be no more weeds. Before planting, it is absolutely essential to make certain that there are no perennial weeds left in the ground. In many cases, even a fragment of root can regrow into a full-sized plant, and no amount of ground cover will prevent this. If perennial weeds do reappear in ground cover there is no alternative but to dig out all of the plants and start again. Therefore, it is important to get the ground completely free of weeds right from the start.

Similarly, if the ground cover is not complete, weeds will simply grow through the gaps. Plants are often recommended as ground cover that are just not dense enough to create total shade at ground level, and such plants are, therefore, useless for ground cover in the horticultural sense. Pinks (*Dianthus*), for example, produce a mat of foliage, but weeds always manage to grow among them. Bear in mind that plants which spread quickly do not necessarily make good ground cover.

VISUAL ADVANTAGES

The other purpose of planting ground cover is to produce a solid mass of one colour as part of a design or colour scheme. For example, a drift of wood anemones (*Anemone nemorosa*) through a wood could be considered ground cover in this context, although the anemones would be useless as weed suppressants.

Allied to this is the use of ground cover plants in order to fill a patch of difficult or unwanted ground. Thus, a drift of *Euphorbia amygdaloides robbiae* could be planted in a dry, shady area to provide some sort of planting because little else would grow there, including the weeds.

When ground cover plants are used, it is often assumed that all the plants should be the same type. This is not completely true. Old-fashioned cottage gardens were often a delightful jumble of plants, planted or self-sown in close proximity. This dense planting still acted as a ground cover, however, even though there was a mixture of different plants. The same principle applies to the modern herbaceous border. Once the clumps of perennials merge in late spring and the ground is covered, the number of weeds that can germinate is greatly reduced. It is only if you leave areas of bare soil showing that you will run into trouble and find that you are constantly having to weed the border.

Left: *The foliage of these hostas provides a very dense ground cover that will help keep weeds at bay, while at the same time looking very attractive.*

DENSE PLANTS FOR MASS GROUND COVER

Acaena
Alchemilla mollis
 (lady's mantle)
Anemone × *hybrida*
 (Japanese anemone)
Bergenia
 (elephant's ears)
Brunnera macrophylla,
 syn. *Anchusa myosotidiflora*
Convallaria majalis
 (lily-of-the-valley)
Crambe cordifolia
Epimedium
Euphorbia
 amygdaloides robbiae
 (wood spurge)
Geranium × *cantabrigiense;*
 G. endressii;
 G. macrorrhizum;
 G. nodosum;
 G. × *oxonianum*

Gunnera
Hosta
Houttuynia cordata
Lysimachia nummularia
 (creeping Jenny)
Maianthemum (may lily)
Persicaria affinis
 (syn. *Polygonum affine*)
Petasites (butterbur,
 sweet coltsfoot)
Pulmonaria (lungwort)
Rheum (ornamental rhubarb)
Rodgersia
Symphytum (comfrey)
Tiarella cordifolia
 (foamflower)
Tolmiea menziesii
 (pickaback plant)
Vancouveria
Vinca minor (lesser
 periwinkle)

Above: Persicaria affinis *provides good ground cover, the flowers (whether in bloom or after they have gone over) as well as the foliage being very attractive for most of the year.*

Above: *The spotted foliage of lungwort* (Pulmonaria) *perfectly sets off the flowers when they appear in late winter and early spring. If sheared over, lungwort will provide excellent ground cover for the rest of the year.*

Above: *The ground-hugging creeping Jenny,* Lysimachia nummularia *'Aurea', works well as a ground cover, as long as all perennial weeds have been removed first.*

Above: *The close planting of any vigorous perennials, such as* Dictamnus, *prevents weed seedlings germinating and surviving.*

Architectural Perennials

Every plant in a border performs a different function or range of functions, contributing to the overall look of the scheme. Some owe their inclusion, at least in part, to their size, shape and sheer physical presence.

USING ARCHITECTURAL PLANTS

Architectural perennials have two roles: one is as individual plants, when they are used to create a focal point, and the other is as a part of the border, when they are used to add to the diversity of shapes and sizes. Focal points in a garden are plants or objects, such as statues or urns, for example, that draw the eye. They can be placed either in isolation – at the end of a path or at the edge of a lawn, for instance – or within a larger arrangement, such as in a border. The eye needs something on which to rest from time to time and one large plant, among many smaller ones, will certainly draw the eye and will probably be the first object the viewer notices.

A cabbage tree (*Cordyline*), for example, with its spray of tapering leaves, placed in an urn at the end of a path will pull your eye towards it so that you appreciate the length and direction of the path. Only afterwards do you draw back and begin to examine the borders on either side of the path. Similarly, a bold architectural perennial, in the middle of a host of other plants in a border, will catch the eye, which rests briefly there, enjoying what it sees, before breaking off and examining the border bit by bit.

On a more general level, a border planted with at least a few architectural perennials is much more interesting than one containing a more uniform planting. Their larger size, as well as the bold shapes of their leaves, adds structure, variety and something striking to look at. However, like most aspects of planting, overdo any one element and the impact is lost.

Strongly shaped perennials often look good in pots or other containers. They can be used in isolation or in groups, and are particularly effective when used as sentinels to a path, steps, a gateway or a door. They also make good plants for patios.

Above: *The biennial or short-lived perennial giant hogweed* (Heracleum mantegazzianum*) is a spectacular plant. However, it should be used with extreme caution as touching it can result in serious skin complaints.*

Left: Gunnera manicata *produces some of the largest leaves seen in gardens. It is bound to catch the eye, wherever it is planted.*

LARGE ARCHITECTURAL PERENNIALS

Acanthus spinosus
  (bear's breeches)
Alcea rosea
  (hollyhock)
Angelica archangelica
  (angelica)
Cordyline australis
  (New Zealand cabbage palm)
Cortaderia selloana
  (pampas grass)
Crambe cordifolia
Cynara cardunculus
  (cardoon)
Delphinium

Gunnera manicata
  (giant rhubarb)
Inula magnifica
Ligularia (leopard plant)
Macleaya cordata
  (plume poppy)
Miscanthus sinensis
Phormium tenax
  (New Zealand flax)
Rheum (ornamental rhubarb)
Stipa gigantea (golden oats)
Telekia speciosa (syn.
  Buphthalmum speciosum)
Verbascum (mullein)

Above: *The red, jagged foliage of the ornamental rhubarb, Rheum 'Ace of Hearts', can be spectacular, particularly when, as here, it is contrasted with more simple foliage.*

Above: *Angelica* (Angelica archangelica*) can be very imposing, but it is a good plant, not only for the herb garden, but also for the wilder parts of the garden.*

Perennials for Foliage

Perennials are often valued purely for the beauty of their flowers. In a well-designed garden, however, their foliage is likely to play an equally important role. Indeed, foliage usually provides the structure and backbone of the whole border, giving greater solidity to the planting scheme.

THE VALUE OF FOLIAGE
If you were to remove all of the foliage from your garden, you would be left with just a few spots of colour. If these spots of colour were seen against one another, or against bare earth, they would not look particularly attractive. However, if you were to place these colours against a sympathetic background of foliage, the picture would be suddenly complete. Foliage helps to bring out the colours in flowers as well as to meld them together.

FOLIAGE SHAPES
Foliage is important because it brings shape, texture and colour to the garden. Of these attributes, shape is the most significant. The strap-shaped leaves of plants such as grasses and irises, for example, have a quite different quality from the large leaves of, say, an ornamental rhubarb (*Rheum*). The shape of a whole plant, which is often dictated by the foliage, also plays a part. Most grasses are tall and often grow in clumps, with the leaves forming the shape of a fountain. Irises, on the other hand, are more upright and have quite a different appearance. Some plants form hummocks; others make flat mats. The interplay of these different shapes is important to the design of a border.

FOLIAGE TEXTURES
Texture is often overlooked in a garden, but it can play a very important role. Plants with shiny leaves, for example, are valuable in shady areas, where they reflect the light, brightening up what would otherwise be a dark corner. On the other hand, velvety leaves absorb the light and give an impression of richness and luxury. There is a world of difference, both in appearance and feel, between the silky leaves of an artemisia and the rough bristles of a gunnera.

FOLIAGE COLOURS
One tends to think of foliage as simply green, but, of course, the range of greens is enormous. In addition, some plants have purple, yellow and even black foliage. These colours can also be variegated in a number of ways. Some are splashed with gold, others with cream; in some the markings are around the edges of the leaves, and in others they are in the centre.

Above: *Light and shadow play beautifully on the foliage of this crocosmia.*

Left: *A group of contrasting foliage shapes, including* Smilacina racemosa *(top left),* Ferula communis *(right) and* Morina afghanica *(bottom left).*

PERENNIALS WITH COLOURED FOLIAGE

PURPLE FOLIAGE

Ajuga reptans
'Atropurpurea';
A. r. 'Burgundy Glow'
Anthriscus sylvestris
'Ravenswing'
Canna 'Roi Humbert'
Clematis recta
'Purpurea'
Cordyline australis
'Atropurpurea'
Dahlia 'Bishop of Llandaff'
Foeniculum vulgare
'Purpureum'
Heuchera micrantha
diversifolia 'Palace Purple'
Ligularia dentata
'Desdemona'; *L. d.* 'Othello'
Lobelia cardinalis
(cardinal flower)
Phormium tenax
Purpureum Group
(New Zealand flax)
Rodgersia aesculifolia;
R. podophylla
Sedum telephium
maximum 'Atropurpureum';
S. 'Morchen';
S. 'Vera Jameson'
Viola riviniana
Purpurea Group
(Labrador violet)

BLUE FOLIAGE

Acaena saccaticupula
'Blue Haze'
(syn. *A.* 'Pewter')
Elymus magellanicus
Festuca glauca
(blue fescue)
Helictotrichon
sempervirens
(syn. *Avena candida*)
Hosta

GOLDEN FOLIAGE

Filipendula ulmaria 'Aurea'
Hosta
Humulus lupulus 'Aureus'
(golden hop)
Lysimachia nummularia
'Aurea'
Milium effusum 'Aureum'
(Bowles' golden grass)
Origanum vulgare 'Aureum'
(golden marjoram)
Phygelius × rectus 'Sunshine'
Tanacetum parthenium
'Aureum' (golden feverfew)

SILVER FOLIAGE

Anaphalis (pearl everlasting)
Artemisia (wormwood);
A. 'Powis Castle'
Celmisia
Cerastium tomentosum
(snow-in-summer)
Convolvulus cneorum
(silverbush)
Cynara cardunculus
(cardoon)
Euphorbia myrsinites;
E. rigida (syn.
E. biglandulosa)
Geranium renardii
Leuzea centauroides
(syn. *Centaurea*
'Pulchra Major')
Lychnis coronaria
Macleaya (plume poppy)
Melianthus major (honeybush)
Romneya coulteri
(Californian poppy)
Santolina
Stachys byzantina;
syn. *S. lanata* (lamb's ears)
Tanacetum haradjanii
Tropaeolum polyphyllum
Verbascum olympicum

Above: *Two contrasting silver foliages: the filigree* Artemisia *'Powis Castle' and the furry* Stachys byzantina.

Right: *The purple foliage of* Anthriscus sylvestris *'Ravenswing', which is overlaid with silver, is strikingly beautiful. Not surprisingly, this plant makes a valuable contribution to many planting schemes.*

Choosing a Colour Scheme

Perennials are available in a wonderful range of colours, which gives gardeners tremendous scope when they design their planting schemes. It is important to remember that colour is provided not only by the flowers, but also by the foliage. The range of colours varies from the bright and brash to the soft and muted. If all these colours were mixed together, without much thought, it would be fun for a while, but the border would soon begin to look untidy and unpleasant to look at.

GROUPING COLOURS

Rather than randomly scattering colours, it is much better to use them in drifts, placing individual plants so that each has a harmonious relationship with its neighbour. When this is done, the eye can move effortlessly along the border, enjoying the subtleties of the border as it passes over a thoughtfully blended whole.

This harmonious relationship depends largely on how different colours relate to each other. Artists and designers use what is known as a colour wheel, in which colours that are situated next to each other on the wheel have a sympathetic bond and will work well together. Purple and blue as well as blue and green, for example, look good together. On the other hand, colours on opposite sides of the wheel are contrasting and may clash with each other. Purple and yellow, for instance, are in stark contrast with each other, and a border in which these two colours are close to one another is likely to be jarring on the eye.

There are, however, occasions when combining opposing colours can be used to create a focal point or to add life to an

Above: *Orange and blue are both powerful colours. Used in together in a planting scheme, they produce an agreeable tension as is shown by these bright blue agapanthus and orange crocosmia.*

Above: *This unusual juxtaposition of purple and brown works very well and emphasizes the advice that you should always be keen to try unusual combinations.*

otherwise bland scheme. A splash of yellow in a purple border, for example, would certainly draw the eye. Red and green are also contrasting colours, and a plant with brilliant red blooms, such as Jerusalem cross (*Lychnis chalcedonica*), can look extraordinarily dramatic against a dark green yew hedge.

Pastel colours have a romantic quality, and are often suitable for a rather dull, grey climate. Even so, a garden devoted entirely to pale colours such as these can be rather boring. Hot colours – the flame reds and oranges – on the other hand, are lively and will bring a dash of excitement to a border.

Unless you have set your heart on a monochromatic border, the basic principle is to blend colours. If you want to use two colours that oppose each other on the colour wheel in close proximity, you can sometimes find another colour that will link them. Blue and red are in stark contrast with each other, and you may prefer to keep them apart by placing a purple plant between them, which will greatly improve the appearance of the border. Incorporating foliage in suitable colours is often an excellent way of linking and separating blocks of colour.

When you are buying plants, always try to see them in flower if you are doubtful about the colour. If the plant is a true variety, its colour should be fixed in most cases, but plants grown from seed can vary greatly in colour. A carefully thought-out colour scheme can be ruined if plants turn out to be pink or white instead of the expected blue, so take care when you are selecting or growing plants.

Right: *Yellow primroses are charmingly set off by their own green foliage and enhanced by a fountain of yellow Bowles' golden grass,* Milium effusum *'Aureum'*.

Below: *The combination of these perennials, including* Sedum telephium maximum *'Atropurpureum' and* Heuchera micrantha diversifolia *'Palace Purple', makes the most of the beautiful subtlety of their colours.*

Hot Colours

Odd as it may seem, colours have temperatures – some colours, like the reds, are regarded as hot, while others, such as the blues, are seen as quite cold. This phenomenon is most noticeable when you are decorating, because the whole mood of a room can change, depending on whether you are using colours based on reds or on blues. It is exactly the same when you are designing and planning a garden.

THE HOT COLOUR PALETTE

The really hot colours are those that are on the orange side of red. They include the flame reds, the oranges and the golden-yellows. Alter the emphasis, and the feeling also changes. For example, yellows that contain a touch of green, rather than orange, are cool. Similarly, reds that contain a lot of blue are not as warm as a lively, hot orange-red, and caution should be used in mixing the two.

It is possible to create a border containing nothing but red flowers, but it is always more interesting to have one that incorporates other hot colours as well. If it suits your personality, you may even want to fill the whole garden with these bright colours. Particularly in a very small garden, where there is not space to create more than one mood, this can produce a very striking effect. However, most people are more comfortable with a balance of hot and cooler areas. Going to a few lively parties is most enjoyable, but go to one every night and they will soon become a bore, and you will be thinking of excuses to stay at home.

Use hot colours with some discretion. Confine them to one border, possibly as a centrepiece,

but use softer colours in the other beds to ring in the changes and to provide a more tranquil planting area. The contrast will be all the stronger, in fact, if the red border is surrounded by less lively colours. However, many people prefer to use a limited number of hot-coloured perennials in the middle of a less adventurous border, where they will act as a strong focal point.

Hot colours also have a tendency to "advance" – that is, they seem much closer than they really are – so if you want to make a long border appear shorter than it is, plant the hot colours at the far end.

Left: *The Chilean glory flower* (Eccremocarpus scaber), *with its bright orange, tubular flowers, can be used to create a splash of colour against a wall or fence.*

Above: *The crimson-red flowers of the flame creeper* (Tropaeolum speciosum) *look very striking as they weave their way over a bright yellow-green conifer.*

PERENNIALS WITH HOT-COLOURED FLOWERS

RED FLOWERS

Canna
Crocosmia 'Lucifer'
Dahlia
Geum 'Mrs J. Bradshaw'
Hemerocallis 'Berlin Red';
 H. 'Ed Murray';
 H. 'Little Red Hen';
 H. 'Red Precious';
 H. 'Stafford'; H. 'Wally
Nance'
Kniphofia (red-hot poker)
Leonotis ocymifolia,
syn. *L. leonurus* (lion's ear)
Lobelia tupa
Lychnis chalcedonica
(Jerusalem cross, Maltese
cross)
Mimulus cupreus
 'Whitecroft Scarlet';
 M. 'Wisley Red'
Monarda 'Cambridge
Scarlet'
Paeonia (peony)
Penstemon barbatus;
P. 'Flame'; P. 'jamesii*;
P. 'Rubicundus'; P. superbus*
Potentilla 'Gibson's Scarlet'
Tropaeolum speciosum
(flame creeper)

ORANGE FLOWERS

Anthemis sancti-johannis
(St John's chamomile)
Canna 'Orange Perfection'
Crocosmia (montbretia);
 C. paniculata*
Dahlia
Eccremocarpus scaber
(Chilean glory flower)
Euphorbia griffithii
Geum 'Borisii';
 G. coccineum*
Hemerocallis (daylily)
Kniphofia (red-hot poker)
Ligularia (leopard plant)
Papaver orientale
(oriental poppy)

Potentilla 'William Rollison'
Primula bulleyana
 (a Candelabra Primula)
Rudbeckia hirta
Trollius (globeflower)
Zauschneria californica

YELLOW–GOLD FLOWERS

Achillea (yarrow);
 A. 'Coronation Gold';
 A. filipendulina* 'Gold Plate'
Anthemis tinctoria
 (golden marguerite)
Aster linosyris
Aurinia saxatilis,
 syn. *Alyssum saxatile*
 (gold dust)
Bupthalmum salicifolium
Canna
Centaurea
 macrocephala
Chrysanthemum
Coreopsis verticillata
Dahlia
Erysimum 'Bredon';
 E. 'Jubilee Gold'
Geum 'Lady Stratheden'
Helenium (sneezeweed)
Helianthus (sunflower)
Heliopsis (ox eye)
Hemerocallis (daylily)
Hieracium (hawkweed)
Inula
Ligularia (leopard plant)
Lysimachia nummularia
 (creeping Jenny);
 L. punctata* (garden
 loosestrife)
Oenothera (evening
 primrose)
Primula
Ranunculus
 (buttercup, crowfoot)
Rudbeckia
 (coneflower)
Solidago (golden rod)
Trollius (globeflower)
Tropaeolum polyphyllum

Right: *Kniphofias have several alternative names, of which red-hot poker aptly describes the colour of many of them. These shafts of hot colours are useful not only for their brightness, but also their shape.*

Below: *The flat flowerheads of Achillea 'Coronation Gold' form a sea of hot yellow, floating above the green foliage.*

Above: Zauschneria californica *has hot orange flowers, but the softness of the foliage tends to take away some of the heat. Soft foliage is often used for this purpose in a border.*

Pastel Colours

If hot colours are jazzy and lively, pastel shades are soft and romantic. They produce a wonderful, hazy effect, which is tranquil and peaceful. The colours in this part of the spectrum include the soft blues, yellows, whites and pinks. They are not the complete opposite of the hot colours, since, in theory, they would simply be the cold or cool colours, but pinks, and those blues that are tinged with red, are warm in temperature. The overall effect, however, is one of cool calm.

COMBINING THE PASTELS

Pastel colours create a misty effect, which means that they can be mixed together and even dotted around. An even better effect can be achieved by using drifts of colour rather than dots, merging or blending one drift into another. Restricting your choice to one specific colour can create an interesting effect, but a border of, for example, only pale blues or pale yellows can look a little wishy-washy, and expanses of these colours should only be used in moderation.

Soft green foliage can provide an effective link in borders and beds filled with pastel colours, whereas dark green, at least in any great quantity, can be too stark. Silver can look stunning when mixed with pinks and pale blue, and, perhaps surprisingly, it can also be extremely effective with pale and greeny yellows. Blue foliage, which can be found in some grasses and hostas, can also be useful in linking or separating blocks of colour.

Many of the pale colours, especially white and blue, stand out well at twilight, and perennials in these colours are particularly useful to plant near an area where you eat in the evening. As the light fades, they will shine out and be seen in ghostly outline, even after it has become quite dark.

Soft, cool colours make objects seem further away, just as, on a misty day, the horizon always seems more distant than it does on a bright day. Designers and gardeners often use this principle in order to make a border seem

Above: Allium christophii *and* Linaria purpurea *'Canon Went' provide a good combination of colours and shapes.*

longer than it actually is, and placing pale colours at the far end of a border creates a surprising optical illusion.

Above: *Using soft yellows and whites together creates a more striking, even starker, contrast than the combination of other pastel shades.*

Right: *Cream, soft mauve and softly variegated foliage blend to create a soothing effect.*

PERENNIALS WITH PALE FLOWERS

BLUE–MAUVE FLOWERS

Aconitum (monkshood;
 this plant is poisonous)
Agapanthus (African lily)
Ajuga reptans (common
 bugle)
Anchusa azurea
Aquilegia flabellata
Aster (Michaelmas daisy)
Baptisia australis
 (blue false indigo)
Brunnera macrophylla,
 syn. *Anchusa myosotidiflora*
Campanula (bellflower)
Catananche caerulea
Delphinium
Echinops ritro
Eryngium (sea holly)
Galega officinalis (goat's rue)
Gentiana (gentian)
Geranium (cranesbill)
Hosta
Iris
Linum narbonense (flax)
Meconopsis (blue poppy)
Myosotis (forget-me-not)
Nepeta (catmint)
Omphalodes (navelwort)
Penstemon heterophyllus
Perovskia atriplicifolia
Platycodon grandiflorus
 (balloon flower)
Polemonium caeruleum
Primula
Pulmonaria (lungwort)
Salvia (sage)
Scabiosa caucasica
Tradescantia × *andersoniana*
Verbena rigida
Veronica (speedwell)

YELLOW FLOWERS

Achillea 'Moonlight'
Anthemis tinctoria 'Sauce
 Hollandaise'
Asphodeline lutea (syn.
 Asphodelus luteus)
Cephalaria gigantea
Coreopsis verticillata
 'Moonbeam'
Digitalis lutea (straw foxglove)
Erysimum suffrutescens
Helenium (sneezeweed)
Helianthus (sunflower)
Heliopsis (ox eye)
Hemerocallis (daylily)
Hieracium (hawkweed)
Iris pseudacorus (yellow flag)
Kniphofia 'Little Maid'
Oenothera stricta 'Sulphurea'
Paeonia mlokosewitschii
Potentilla recta
Primula
Ranunculus (buttercup,
 crowfoot)
× *Solidaster luteus*
Thalictrum flavum glaucum
Trollius × *cultorum* 'Alabaster'

PINK FLOWERS

Anemone × *hybrida*
 (Japanese anemone)
Armeria (thrift, sea pink)
Aster (Michaelmas daisy)
Astilbe
Bergenia cordifolia
Dianthus (carnations, pinks)
Diascia
Dicentra
Erigeron 'Charity'
Filipendula (meadowsweet)
Geranium (cranesbill)
Lamium maculatum 'Roseum'
Linaria purpurea 'Canon Went'
Lychnis flos-jovis
Malva moschata (musk
 mallow)
Monarda 'Croftway Pink'
Penstemon 'Hidcote Pink'
Persicaria (knotweed)
Phlox paniculata (perennial
 phlox)
Phuopsis stylosa
Primula
Sedum (stonecrop)
Sidalcea (prairie mallow)

Above. *Pink is a very good colour to use in pastel schemes. These pinks (Dianthus) are a particularly good choice because they often have a soft, romantic perfume as well.*

Above: *Mauves and silvers in the foreground combine with other soft colours to create a tranquil cottage garden.*

White and Cream Perennials

White is a symbolic colour, and, since the earliest days of gardening, white flowers have had a special significance. Many gardeners are sufficiently under its spell to devote whole borders to the colour. White imparts a sense of purity and tranquillity, and these are two of the qualities that flowers of this colour will bring to a garden. There is something serene about an area of white flowers that is difficult to capture in any other way. It is a good idea to place a seat in an area devoted to white flowers, because it is the perfect place in which to relax.

THE WHITE GARDEN

In has become fashionable to devote whole borders, even whole gardens, to white flowers. Although they are usually referred to as white gardens, there are usually at least two colours present, because most white-flowered plants have green leaves. A third colour, in the form of grey or silver foliage, is also often added.

It is not as easy as it may seem to create a white garden, because there are, perhaps surprisingly, many different shades of white, and they do not always mix sympathetically. On the whole, it is better to stick to pure whites, since the creamier ones tend to "muddy" the picture. Creams are soothing in themselves, and, with care, a border can be created from them, as an alternative to pure white. Many white and cream flowers, particularly members of the daisy family, have bright yellow centres, and it best to avoid these if you are planning a white border. They do, however, mix better with cream flowers.

White and cream go well with most other colours, and they can be used to lighten a colour scheme. When used with hot oranges and reds, pure white can create a dramatic effect, whereas creams add a slightly mellower feel. White and blue is always a popular combination, and it can be particularly effective to combine different shades of white and cream with a mixture of pastel colours. White is visible until well after dark, and so it is a good colour to plant where you eat evening meals.

Above: *Planting* Arabis alpina caucasica *'Flore Pleno' against the dark purple-brown foliage of* Euphorbia dulcis *'Chameleon' accentuates the whiteness of the flowers.*

Left: *An association of white* Tanacetum parthenium *with* Galega × hartlandii *'Alba'. The yellow centres of the tanacetum flowers soften the stark effect of having so many white-flowers.*

WHITE AND CREAM PERENNIALS

Achillea ptarmica 'The Pearl'
Aconitum napellus vulgare
 'Albidum' (poisonous)
Agapanthus campanulatus
 albidus
Anaphalis margaritacea
Anemone × *hybrida*
 'Honorine Jobert';
 A. nemorosa (wood anemone)
Anthemis punctata cupaniana
Anthericum liliago
 (St Bernard's lily)
Aquilegia vulgaris 'Nivea'
Arabis (rock cress)
Argyranthemum frutescens
 (marguerite)
Artemisia lactiflora (white
 mugwort)
Aruncus dioicus (goat's
 beard)
Aster novae-angliae
 'Herbstschnee'
Astilbe × *arendsii* 'Irrlicht'
Bellis (daisy)
Bergenia 'Silberlicht'
Campanula latiloba 'Alba'
Centranthus ruber 'Albus'
Cerastium tomentosum
 (snow-in-summer)
Cimicifuga cordifolia;
 C. simplex
Convallaria majalis
 (lily-of-the-valley)
Crambe cordifolia
Dianthus 'Haytor White';
 D. 'Mrs Sinkins'
Dicentra spectabilis 'Alba'
Dictamnus albus
Echinops sphaerocephalus
Epilobium angustifolium
 album
Eryngium eburneum
Galium odoratum, syn.
 Asperula odorata (woodruff)
Geranium phaeum 'Album';
 G. sanguineum 'Album'
Gypsophila paniculata
 'Bristol Fairy'
Hosta

Houttuynia cordata
Iberis sempervirens
Iris
Lamium maculatum
 'White Nancy'
Leucanthemum × *superbum*
 'Everest'
Lilium (lily)
Lupinus (lupin)
Lychnis coronaria 'Alba'
Lysimachia clethroides
 (gooseneck loosestrife);
 L. ephemerum
Malva moschata alba
 (white musk mallow)
Myrrhis odorata (sweet cicely)
Osteospermum ecklonis
Paeonia (peony)
Papaver orientale
 'Perry's White'
Penstemon serrulatus 'Albus';
 P. 'White Bedder'
Phlox paniculata 'Fujiyama'
Physostegia virginiana 'Alba'
Polygonatum × *hybridum*
 (syn. *P. multiflorum*)
Pulmonaria officinalis
 'Sissinghurst White'
Ranunculus aconitifolius
 (bachelor's buttons)
Rodgersia
Romneya coulteri
 (Californian poppy)
Sanguinaria canadensis
 (bloodroot)
Silene uniflora, syn.
 S. maritima (sea campion)
Smilacina racemosa (false
 spikenard); *S. stellata*
 (star flower)
Thalictrum (meadow rue)
Trillium grandiflorum
 (wake robin)
Verbascum chaixii 'Album'
Veronica gentianoides 'Alba'
Viola cornuta Alba Group;
 V. odorata 'Alba'
Zantedeschia aethiopica
 (arum lily)

Above: *The flowers of* Crambe cordifolia *create a white haze, a quite different effect from that produced by plants with more "solid" flowers.*

Above: *The clusters of small flowers of* Eupatorium album *'Braunlaub' produce a foam-like effect, rather like waves breaking on a seashore.*

Spring

Although the working year in the garden begins in winter, it is spring that heralds the start of the new flowering season. Because most perennials are herbaceous, they have spent time below ground and now emerge as clumps of new foliage. Some plants, however, will have been around all winter. The lungworts (*Pulmonaria*), for example, have been in leaf constantly and now produce masses of blue, red, pink or white flowers. The hellebores are in full swing, as are the primulas, of which the humble primrose (*Primula vulgaris*) is still one of the best loved.

SPRING COLOURS

As the days begin to lengthen and the air and ground become warmer, the early-comers, such as hellebores, winter aconites and primulas, move into the background as other plants begin to emerge. Indeed, it is a good idea to grow the early plants towards the back of the bed or border so that they show up in early spring, when they are in flower, but then disappear behind later-flowering plants for the rest of the year. Among the next phase of plants are the bleeding hearts (*Dicentra spectabilis*) and other dicentras, which need light shade and will grow happily under trees that have yet to open their leaves. Wood anemones (*Anemone nemorosa*), which are available in a range of white and delicate blues, pinks and yellows, also make use of the temporary light under deciduous trees and shrubs.

At this time of year everything feels fresh. The soil is often still damp, and the foliage and flowers are brightly coloured. One of the most ubiquitous colours of spring is sunny yellow. Apart from bulbs such as crocuses and daffodils, many perennials put in an appearance, including leopard's bane (*Doronicum*), with its brilliant golden daisies, and kingcups (*Caltha*), which are a must for any bog or waterside planting. *Paeonia mlokosewitschii*, one of the earliest peonies to flower, has delicate yellow flowers (which are followed in autumn by scarlet and black seeds). This

Left: *The bright yellow flowers of* Anemone ranunculoides *'Pleniflora' can be used to illuminate a shady spot.*

Above: Euphorbia polychroma *creates a perfect dome, which is effective in any spring border.*

yellow is intensified in association with the acid green of *Euphorbia polychroma*, which forms beautiful mounds.

LATE SPRING FLOURISHES

As spring passes, the number of plants in leaf and flower increases, until, just on the juncture with early summer, the garden almost seems over-burdened and it is difficult to keep pace with the newcomers. At this time of year, the foliage also still looks crisp and lush, before the strong sun drains away its colour and freshness.

Many gardeners like to plant in spring, but it is important not to get too carried away and to plant only those plants that are in flower or of interest at the time. Remember to include some that will provide something to look at later in the year.

Above: *Primroses are ideal for a cottage garden.*

Below: *The purple foliage and blue flowers of* Veronica peduncularis *'Georgia Blue' form spectacular spring carpets.*

SPRING-FLOWERING PERENNIALS

Ajuga reptans
 (common bugle)
Anemone blanda;
 A. nemorosa (wood anemone)
Arabis (rock cress)
Bergenia (elephant's ears)
Cardamine (bitter cress)
Dicentra
Doronicum (leopard's bane)
Erythronium
 (dog's-tooth violet)
Euphorbia polychroma
Helleborus (hellebore)
Lamium maculatum; L. orvala

Meconopsis cambrica
 (Welsh poppy)
Myosotis (forget-me-not)
Primula
Pulmonaria (lungwort)
Pulsatilla
 (pasqueflower)
Ranunculus ficaria
 (lesser celandine)
Symphytum (comfrey)
Trillium (wood lily)
Veronica peduncularis
 'Georgia Blue'
Viola

Right: *The delicate flowers of dicentras bring freshness to a spring border. Here, they are planted with forget-me-nots.*

Summer

Summer always seems to arrive unannounced. One minute it is spring, the next it is summer, and the borders are bursting with life. Summer is the height of the perennial year. It is a season of colour and scents, humming bees and fluttering butterflies. It is also a time when gardeners should be able to relax and enjoy the fruits of their labours.

THE STAGES OF SUMMER

Although this season is usually regarded simply as "summer", in gardening terms there is quite a difference between early summer, midsummer and late summer. Early summer carries on where spring left off, with plenty of fresh-looking foliage and bright colours. Lupins, poppies, peonies and delphiniums add to the delights and are vital parts of any display at this time of year.

As midsummer approaches, the colours change subtly and flowers with more muted tones unfurl, including *Catananche* (sometimes known as cupid's dart), penstemons, baby's breath (*Gypsophila*) and phlox.

By late summer the colours are fading and the foliage is starting to look a little tired. The colours begin to swing towards the autumnal ones of deep golds and russet reds, as perennials such as achilleas, heleniums and inulas come into their own.

There are perennials with flowers in all colours throughout the summer, and so you can control the appearance of the borders by choosing whatever colours you need. Some plants flower throughout the season – various hardy geraniums, for example, will supply colour for months on end, and a number of red-hot pokers (*Kniphofia*) can supply displays of red and orange spikes throughout the entire summer and well into the autumn.

BED AND BORDER CARE

As the display changes, it is important that the beds and borders are kept tidy and well-maintained, so that dead and dying material does not mar the appearance of what is currently in flower. The flowers of each plant should be dead-headed as soon as they go over. This not only removes an eyesore, but also prevents the plant's energy from being spent on seed production. Instead, the energy is channelled back into the plant, which may then produce a second, later crop of flowers.

Some plants benefit from being cut right back to the ground, which encourages a flush of new leaves, so they can then act as foliage plants. Lady's mantle (*Alchemilla mollis*), for example, not only looks tired and tatty if it is left, but it also seeds itself everywhere. If it is sheared back to its base after flowering, however, it will produce a set of beautiful new foliage and self-sowing will have been prevented.

Although constant attention to the borders is needed to keep them looking their best, there is little point in producing a magnificent garden if you do not allow yourself any time to relax in it and admire the results of all your labours. Make a point of strolling around your garden, perhaps in company, or, better still, sit back and simply admire what you have achieved. Your garden will more than repay the effort you have put into it.

Left: *This cottage garden, shown in early summer, is full of freshness and vitality, as the borders begin to fill out with lush vegetation and flowers.*

Above: *The hardy geraniums are one of the mainstays of the summer border. There is a vast range from which to choose.*

Above: *The achilleas with their flat heads bring an air of calm as well as a splash of bright colour to the summer border.*

SUMMER-FLOWERING PERENNIALS

Acanthus (bear's breeches)	*Hemerocallis* (daylily)
Achillea (yarrow)	*Heuchera* (coral bells)
Aconitum (monkshood; this plant is poisonous)	*Hosta*
Alchemilla (lady's mantle)	*Inula*
Aster amellus; *A. × frikartii*	*Iris*
Astilbe	*Kniphofia* (red-hot poker)
Baptisia (false indigo)	*Leucanthemum*
Campanula (bellflower)	*Ligularia* (leopard plant)
Catananche (cupid's dart, blue cupidone)	*Lilium* (lily)
Centaurea (knapweed)	*Lupinus* (lupin)
Dianthus (carnations, pinks)	*Macleaya* (plume poppy)
Digitalis (foxglove; this plant is poisonous)	*Monarda* (bergamot)
Echinops (globe thistle)	*Paeonia* (peony)
Erigeron (fleabane)	*Papaver* (poppy)
Eryngium (sea holly)	*Penstemon*
Euphorbia (spurge, milkweed)	*Phlox*
Geranium (cranesbill)	*Rodgersia*
Gypsophila (baby's breath)	*Scabiosa* (scabious, pincushion flower)
Helenium (sneezeweed)	*Stachys*
	Veronica (speedwell)
	Viola

Above: *Perennial varieties of wallflower (*Erysimum*) make colourful subjects for the early summer border, but, unfortunately, they are not perfumed like the ones treated as annual bedding plants.*

Above: *This summer border, with its delightful combination of fresh yellows and greens and the addition of some bright red highlights, has been beautifully planted.*

Autumn

Apart from looking at the calendar, it is not always possible to say when autumn starts in the garden. High summer usually slips quietly into autumn and there is little apparent change, but, as winter approaches, the differences become much more noticeable.

AUTUMN HUES

Autumn can be a beautiful month in the garden. The colours may be becoming more muted, but there are still plenty of bright tones left. Many plants run on into the autumn from earlier seasons – the penstemons and Japanese anemones (*Anemone* × *hybrida*), for example – but true autumn has its own distinctive flora. The Michaelmas daisies (*Aster*) are one of the mainstays of the autumn garden, as are the chrysanthemums, while ice plants and stonecrops (*Sedum*) are invaluable for attracting the last of the butterflies and bees.

Yellows and oranges are quite common at this time of year, with the coneflowers (*Rudbeckia*) and sunflowers (*Helianthus*) in flower, but there are also deep purple ironweeds (*Vernonia*) and Michaelmas daisies to add variety.

Lilyturf (*Liriope*), with its blue spikes of berry-like flowers, is a good autumn plant. It is useful because it is one of the few autumn-flowering plants that will grow in shade. The toad lily (*Tricyrtis*) and kirengeshoma, which bloom in late summer and early autumn, are also well worth growing. Many grasses are at their best in autumn, especially the large, statuesque pampas grasses (*Cortaderia*) and miscanthus.

AUTUMN MAINTENANCE

It is important to keep on top of maintenance at this time of year. A general lassitude often seems to set in and maintenance tasks are left to the winter. Unfortunately, the dead material often masks plants that are still flowering, so if dead and dying plants are cleared away regularly, the autumn border will look all the better. A few dead stems add to the beauty of the autumn and winter border, however, and the dead stems and seedheads of the sea hollies (*Eryngium*), in particular, are well worth leaving.

If you are planning a major replanting of a border, it is often worth sacrificing a couple of weeks' flowering, so that you can start work on the border in the autumn. This will give the ground an opportunity to weather and any remaining weeds that reappear can be dealt with before planting begins in spring.

Above: *Autumn is a time of rich golds, as this* Rudbeckia fulgida deamii *shows. Its appearance is a reminder that the gardening year is coming to an end.*

Left: *Many of the autumn-flowering sedums are doubly valuable, working well as foliage plants in the summer, before their softly textured flowers emerge in autumn.*

Above: *Autumn-flowering sedums are excellent for attracting late flying butterflies and bees as well as providing colour for the border.*

Above: *There are a number of autumn bulbs that are usually regarded as perennials. This beautiful, but nearly unpronounceable,* Schizostylus coccinea *is one of them.*

Right: *Asters are one of the mainstays of autumn. However, some, such as this* Aster × frikartii *'Mönch', flower over a very long period, from midsummer right through to late autumn.*

AUTUMN-FLOWERING PERENNIALS

Anemone × hybrida
 (Japanese anemone)
Aster (Michaelmas daisy)
Boltonia
Chelone (turtle head)
Chrysanthemum
Cimicifuga (bugbane)
Helianthus (sunflower)
Kirengeshoma
 palmata
Liriope (lilyturf)

Leucanthemella serotina
Nerine (this is a bulb)
Ophiopogon
Rudbeckia (coneflower)
Schizostylis coccinea
 (Kaffir lily; this is a bulb)
Sedum (stonecrop); *S. spectabile*
 (ice-plant)
Solidago (golden rod)
Tricyrtis (toad lily)
Vernonia (ironweed)

Winter

Many gardeners like to hibernate in the winter, not poking their noses out into the garden until the worst of the weather is over. This is a mistake. Not only is there plenty to see and enjoy in the garden at this time of year, but an hour's work done now is worth several later on.

A WINTER GARDEN

Several plants flower in the winter, including a number of perennials. Although it might not be a good idea to fill busy summer borders with them, they can still be grown at the back of the bed where they will emerge later, while remaining hidden during the summer. If you have the space, it is a good idea to create a "winter garden" where you can enjoy these plants in an area specially devoted to them.

If you can, plant beneath deciduous trees and shrubs, where there is plenty of light during the perennials' growing season, but where they will be out of sight for the rest of the year. Even under-planting a single bush will create a small winter garden.

WINTER PERENNIALS

Hellebores (*Helleborus*) are one of the mainstays of the perennial scene in winter. Perhaps they would not be so important if they flowered later in the year, but their flowers are most welcome during the winter months. They are available in a wide range of colours, and there are also an increasing number of double varieties. *Helleborus purpurascens* is the earliest to flower, usually appearing before midwinter, but the so-called Christmas rose (*H. niger*) usually flowers later than this.

One doesn't normally expect irises to be in flower in winter, but the Algerian iris (*Iris unguicularis*) starts flowering in late autumn and goes on until early spring, taking little notice of the weather. Its mauve or purple flowers are deliciously scented. It also grows best in

Above: *Many perennials, such as this houseleek (*Sempervivum*) growing on the roof of a porch, are evergreen, which makes them very useful for providing winter decoration and interest.*

Above: *Winter aconites (*Eranthis hyemalis*) are true harbingers of spring. Once they have pushed up through the ground, sometimes even in the snow, you know that winter is almost over.*

poor soil and is a particularly good plant to grow in rocky soil near the house. It is, however, irresistible to slugs, and these should be kept at bay if you want flowers. It is the only winter plant that needs an open position.

The lungworts (*Pulmonaria*) are really spring flowers, but in most years they will flower in winter as well, sometimes in early winter. Primroses (*Primula vulgaris*) often flower sporadically at this time of year, too, and sweet violets (*Viola odorata*) will flower in warm spots, often providing an indoor display for early winter.

WINTER-FLOWERING PERENNIALS

Anemone nemorosa
 (wood anemone)
Eranthis hyemalis
 (winter aconite)
Euphorbia rigida
Helleborus niger
 (Christmas rose);
 H. orientalis (Lenten rose);
 H. purpurascens
Iris unguicularis
 (Algerian iris)
Primula vulgaris
 (primrose)
Pulmonaria rubra
 (lungwort)
Viola odorata (sweet violet)

Above right: *Wood anemones* (Anemone nemorosa) *come through the soil before anything else is stirring, and briefly clothe the ground with leaves and flowers.*

Right: *Many varieties of hellebores and pulmonarias start to flower very early in the year, often before midwinter.*

PLANT LISTS

For all gardeners, making the right selection of plants is the single most important ingredient for successful gardening. To do this, you must be informed on several different levels: you need to be able to identify the overall look you are hoping to achieve and the kind of garden you want to create, and you also need to understand the conditions that determine which plants will grow successfully. Perhaps the most important lesson for any novice gardener is to grasp that you cannot grow exactly what you want wherever you please. Although you always want to try and manage nature, or at least influence it as much as you dare, the most successful gardeners are those who look at how plants grow in their natural habitat, and apply this to their own garden, working with nature wherever possible. The greater your understanding of where plants grow best, and what their individual needs are, the easier it becomes to grow them.

Left: *Dahlias make excellent cut flowers and can be grown in a general border, as here, or in a separate plot.*

Annuals List

Choose from this list of annuals for specific purposes such as lime or chalk (alkaline) soil.

YELLOW-FLOWERED ANNUALS

Argemone mexicana
Calendula officinalis 'Kablouna'
Chrysanthemum segetum
Chrysanthemum tenuiloba 'Golden Fleck'
Coreopsis 'Sunray'
Glaucium flavum
Helianthus annuus
Limnanthes douglasii
Lonas annua
Oenothera biennis
Sanvitalia procumbens
Tagetes 'Gold Coins'

Chrysanthemum segetum *and* Dahlia *'David Howard"*

ORANGE FLOWERED ANNUALS

Alonsoa warscewiczii
Calceolaria 'Kentish Hero'
Emilia coccinea
Erysimum cheiri 'Fire King'
Impatiens 'Impact Orange'
Nemesia 'Orange Prince'
Osteospermum hyoseroides 'Gaiety'
Rudbeckia hirta 'Goldilocks'
Tithonia rotundifolia 'Torch'
Tropaeolum majus 'Alaska'

Papaver rhoeas *'Mother of Pearl'*

RED FLOWERED ANNUALS

Amaranthus caudatus
Antirrhinum 'Scarlet Giant'
Begonia semperflorens 'Lucifer'
Cosmos bipinnatus 'Pied Piper Red'
Dianthus chinensis 'Fire Carpet'
Impatiens 'Tempo Scarlet'
Lathyrus odoratus 'Airwarden'
Lobelia erinus 'Red Cascade'
Nicotiana 'Crimson'
Papaver rhoeas
Petunia 'Red Star'
Tagetes patula 'Cinnabar'
Tropaeolum majus 'Empress of India'
Verbena 'Sandy Scarlet'

PINK FLOWERED ANNUALS

Alcea rosea 'Rose'
Begonia semperflorens 'Pink Avalanche'
Callistephus chinensis
Cleome 'Pink Queen'
Cosmos 'Versailles Tetra'
Crepis rubra
Clarkia grandiflora 'Satin Pink'
Helichrysum bracteatum 'Rose'
Lavatera trimestris 'Pink Beauty'
Nicotiana 'Domino Salmon-Pink'
Oenothera speciosa
Osteospermum 'Lady Leitrim'
Papaver somniferum

BLUE FLOWERED ANNUALS

Borago officinalis
Campanula medium
Centaurea cyanus
Consolida ambigua
Echium vulgare
Limonium sinuatum 'Azure'
Myosotis
Nemophila menziesii
Nicandra physalodes
Nigella damascena
Salvia farinacea 'Victoria'

Osteospermum hyoseroides

Cloeme hassleriana

PURPLE AND VIOLET FLOWERED ANNUALS

Ageratum 'North Star'
Antirrhinum 'Purple King'
Centaurea cyanus 'Black Ball'
Eschscholzia californica 'Purple-Violet'
Galactites tomentosa
Heliotropium
Hesperis matronalis
Limonium sinuatum 'Midnight'

Osteospermum *'Tresco Purple'*

Nigella damascena *'Miss Jekyll'*

Lunaria annua
Senecio ciliocarpa
Silene armeria 'Electra'
Trachelium caeruleum

WHITE AND CREAM-FLOWERED ANNUALS
Antirrhinum 'White Wonder'
Argemone grandiflora
Centaurea moschata 'The Bride'
Clarkia pulchella
  'Snowflake'
Digitalis purpurea alba
Gypsophila elegans 'White
  Elephant'
Hibiscus trionum
Iberis crenata
Lobularia maritima
Nemesia 'Mellow White'
Nemophila maculata
Nicotiana sylvestris
Osteospermum
  'Prostratum'
Tagetes 'French Vanilla'

ANNUALS FOR LIME OR CHALKY SOIL
Ageratum houstonianum
Calendula officinalis
Callistephus chinensis
Chrysanthemum
Erysimum
Gypsophila

Digitalis purpurea alba

Lavatera trimestris 'Silver Cup'
Limonium sinuatum
Lobularia maritima
Matthiola
Salvia viridis
Tagetes
Zinnia

ANNUALS FOR SANDY SOIL
Antirrhinum majus
Brachycome iberidifolia
Coreopsis tinctoria
Dimorphotheca
Helichrysum bracteatum
Limnanthes douglasii
Limonium sinuatum
Lobularia maritima
Mesembryanthemum
Papaver rhoeas
Schizanthus
Tagetes
Tropaeolum

Lunaria annua variegata

Nasturtiums with Tagetes *'Suzie Wong'*

Tagetes patula *'Safari Tangerine'*

Amaranthus

ANNUALS WITH FRAGRANT FLOWERS
Brachycome iberidifolia
Centaurea moschata
Dianthus barbatus
Erysimum
Heliotropium
Iberis umbellata
Lathyrus odoratus
Limnanthes douglasii
Lobularia maritima
Matthiola incana
Nicotiana alata
Oenothera biennis
Reseda odorata
Scabiosa atropurpurea

ANNUALS WITH SCENTED FOLIAGE
Salvia sclarea

ANNUALS FOR CUT FLOWERS
Amaranthus caudatus
Callistephus chinensis
Centaurea cyanus
Centaurea moschata
Gypsophila elegans
Helipterum roseum
Lathyrus odoratus

Salvia sclarea *var.* turkestanica

Limonium sinuatum
Matthiola
Moluccella laevis
Zinnia elegans

ANNUALS FOR DRIED FLOWERS
Amaranthus caudatus
Centaurea cyanus
Gypsophila elegans
Helichrysum bracteatum
Limonium sinuatum
Moluccella laevis
Onopordum acanthium
Salvia viridis
Scabiosa atropurpurea

Osteospermum ecklonis *var.* prostratum

ANNUALS FOR FOLIAGE

Abutilon megapotamicum
  'Variegatum'
Atriplex hortensis 'Rubra'
Beta vulgaris
Brassica oleracea
Canna
Coleus blumei
Euphorbia marginata
Helichrysum petiolare
Medicago echinus
Melianthus major
Onopordum acanthium
Ricinus communis
Senecio cineraria
Tropaeolum majus 'Alaska'

ANNUALS FOR EXPOSED AND COASTAL SITES

Antirrhinum majus
Calendula officinalis
Clarkia amoena
Coreopsis tinctoria
Eschscholzia californica
Helichrysum bracteatum
Limnanthes douglasii
Matthiola
Tagetes

ANNUAL CLIMBERS

Asarina erubescens
Cobaea scandens
Convolvulus tricolor

Zinnia *Giant Double mixed with* Tithonia rotundifolia *'Torch'*

Canna *'Wyoming' and 'Striata'*, Ricinus communis *'Zanzibariensis' and mixed* Dahlias *'Rigoletto'*

Early chrysanthemums with Helianthus *'Valentine' and* Eupatorium purpureum

Perennials List

A list of perennials for specific purposes such as colour schemes and particular soils.

YELLOW-FLOWERED PERENNIALS
Achillea 'Coronation Gold'
Anemone ranunculoides 'Plentiflora'
Caltha palustris
Doronicum
Eranthis hyemalis
Helianthus
Kirengeshoma palmata
Lysimachia punctata
Milium effusum 'Aureum'
Paeonia mlokosewitschii
Rudbeckia
Solidago
Verbascum olympicum

ORANGE-FLOWERED PERENNIALS
Asclepias tuberosa
Eccremocarpus scaber
Euphorbia griffithii 'Fireglow'
Helenium 'Wyndley'
Hemerocallis 'Golden Chimes'
Kniphofia caulescens
Kniphofia triangularis
Strelitzia reginae
Zauschneria californica

RED-FLOWERED PERENNIALS
Astilbe 'Montgomery'
Cosmos atrosanguineus
Kohleria eriantha
Lobelia 'Cherry Ripe'

Doronicum

Lychnis chalcedonica
Monarda bradburyana 'Cambridge Scarlet'
Papaver orientale
Rheum palmatum 'Atrosanguineum'
Schizostylis coccinea 'Major'
Tropaeolum speciosum

Meconopsis

PINK-FLOWERED PERENNIALS
Anemone huphensis
Astilbe arendsii 'Venus'
Centaurea pucherrima
Dicentra spectabilis
Eupatorium purpureum
Filipendula rubra
Lupinus 'The Chatelaine'
Mirabilis jalapa
Salvia involucrata
Schizostylis coccinea 'Sunrise'
Sedum spectabile
Tanacetum coccineum 'Brenda'

BLUE-FLOWERED PERENNIALS
Agapanthus 'Dorothy Palmer'
Agapanthus praecox orientalis
Aster × frikartii 'Mönch'
Convolvulus sabatius
Gentiana asclepiadea
Mertensia pulmonarioides
Pulmonaria angustifolia
Veronica peduncularis 'Georgia Blue'

PURPLE-AND-VIOLET FLOWERED PERENNIALS
Acanthus spinosus
Campanula lactiflora 'Prichard's Variety'
Clematis 'Etoile Violette'
Geranium phaeum
Helleborus purpurascens
Heuchera micrantha 'Palace Purple'
Iris unguicularis
Liriope muscari
Monarda fistulosa
Verbena patagonica

WHITE-AND-CREAM FLOWERED PERENNIALS
Anaphalis margaritacea
Anemone nemorosa
Caltha introloba
Convallaria majalis
Crambe cordifolia
Dicentra spectabilis 'Alba'
Dictamnus albus
Eupatorium album 'Braunlaub'
Galium odoratum
Gypsophila paniculata

Liriope muscari

Euphorbia griffithii *'Fireglow'*

Tropaeolum speciosum

Convallaria majalis

Helleborus niger
Ranunculus aconitifolius
Rodgersia podophylla
Salvia argentea
Tanacetum parthenium

GREEN-FLOWERED PERENNIALS
Alchemilla mollis
Euphorbia amygdaloides
   var. *robbiae*
Euphorbia cyparissias
Euphorbia polychroma
Kniphofia 'Percy's Bride'
Thalictrum lucidum

PERENNIALS FOR DRY SHADE
Alchemilla mollis
Brunnera
Euphorbia amygdaloides
   var. *robbiae*
Iris foetidissima
Kohleria digitaliflora
Streptocarpus saxorum
Tradescantia zebrina
   'Quadricolor'
Viola

PERENNIALS FOR MOIST SHADE
Aconitum
Anemone × hybrida
Aruncus dioicus
Bergenia
Convallaria majalis
Digitalis orientalis
Helleborus foetidus
Helleborus niger
Helleborus orientalis
Hosta

Eupatorium purpureum

Clematis *'Etoile Violette'*

Helleborus orientalis *hybrid*

Ligularia
Ranunculus
Rodgersia

PERENNIALS FOR ACID SOIL
Cypripedium reginae
Drosera
Liriope
Lupinus
Meconopsis
Nepenthes
Sarracenia flava
Trillium
Uvularia

PERENNIALS FOR ALKALINE OR LIME SOIL
Acanthus spinosus
Achillea filipendulina
  'Gold Plate'
Alyssum
Aubrietia
Bergenia
Campanula
Dianthus
Doronicum
Erysimum
Gypsophila paniculata
Salvia nemorosa

Campanula Latiloba *'Percy Piper'*

Scabiosa
Verbascum

PERENNIALS FOR SANDY SOIL
Acanthus spinosus
Alstroemeria
Cryptanthus zonatus
Eryngium × tripartitu
Limonium latifolium

PERENNIALS FOR CLAY SOIL
Aruncus dioicus
Filipendula ulmaria 'Aurea'
Gunnera manicata
Houttuynia cordata
  'Chameleon'
Iris laevigata
Mimulus guttatus
Trollius

PERENNIALS FOR GROUNDCOVER
Alchemilla mollis
Anemone nemerosa
Artemisia frigida

Euphorbia polychroma *'Major'*

Dianthus deltoides
Euphorbia amygdaloides
  var. *robbiae*
Geranium macrorrhizum
Hosta
Lysimachia nummularia
  'Aurea'
Osteospermum jucundum
Persicaria affinis
Pulmonaria
Stachys byzantina

Helleborus × nigercors

Viola

Dianthus *'Haytor White'*

PERENNIALS WITH FRAGRANT FLOWERS
Convallaria majalis
Cosmos atrosanguineus
Dianthus
Galium odoratum
Hesperis matronalis
Iris graminea
Lupinus
Nicotiana sylvestris
Phlox maculata

Saponaria officinalis
Sedum spectabile
Verbena × hybrida 'Defiance'

PERENNIALS WITH SCENTED FOLIAGE
Agastache mexicana
Artemisia alba 'Canescens'
Cestrum parqui
Galium odoratum
Geranium macrorrhizum

Houttuynia cordata
'Chameleon'
Meum
Nepeta cataria
Pelargonium quercifolium
Tanacetum parthenium

PERENNIALS FOR CUT FLOWERS
Anaphalis
Astrantia major
Chrysanthemum
Helleborus niger
Phlox paniculata
Strelitzia reginae

PERENNIALS FOR DRIED FLOWERS
Astilbe
Catananche caerulea 'Major'
Echinops
Gypsophila paniculata
Limonium
Lythrum
Rodgersia
Solidago
Typha

ARCHITECTURAL PERENNIALS
Angelica archangelica
Cordyline
Gunnera manicata
Heracleum mantegazzianum
Rheum 'Ace of Hearts'

PERENNIALS FOR FOLIAGE
Anthriscus sylvestris
'Ravenswing'
Artemisia 'Powis Castle'
Crocosmia
Euphorbia mellifera
Ferula communis
Morina afghanica
Osmunda regalis
Phormium tenax
Stachys byzantina

Alstroemeria ligtu *hybrids with* Lychnis coronaria

PERENNIALS FOR COASTAL AND EXPOSED SITES
Anaphalis margaritacea
Anthurium andraeanum
Echinacea purpurea
Erigeron 'Charity'
Euphorbia griffithii 'Fireglow'
Kniphofia caulescens
Phormium tenax
Salvia argentea
Senecio cineraria 'Silver Dust'

PERENNIAL CLIMBERS
Clematis
Eccremocarpus scaber
Tropaeolum speciosum
Vinca major

PERENNIALS FOR HEDGES
Echinops bannaticus
Helianthus atrorubens
'Monarch'
Macleaya microcarpa
'Coral Plume'
Rudbeckia 'Goldquelle'

Hosta *'Gold Standard'*

INDEX

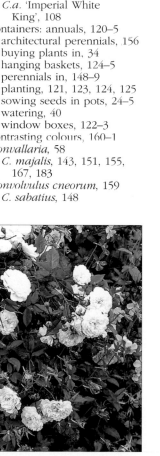

ACKNOWLEDGEMENTS

The publishers would like to thank the following for their permission to photograph their plants and gardens for this book: Hilary and Richard Bird; the RHS Garden, Wisley; Mavis and David Seeney; and Merriments Gardens, Kent.

The publishers would also like to thank the following photographers and picture agencies for allowing their pictures to be reproduced in this book:

KEY: t = top b = bottom l = left r = right

Richard Bird for the pictures on pages 48 (all) and 49br.

Jonathan Buckley for the pictures on pages 18, 24bl, 25br, 41br, 531br, 58, 62 (all),128, 129, 135 (all), 142r, 147 (all), 162 (all), 172 (all), 173(all), 174(all), 175(all), 176 (all), 177(all), 178 (all), 179 (all), 180(all), 181(all), 182 (all), 183 (all), 184(all), 185 (all) 186 (all) 187 (all) 188 (all) 189 (all)190(all)191 (all) 192 (all).

The Garden Picture Library for the pictures on pages 29r (Brigitte Thomas), 29br (JS Sira), 41r (Howard Rice) 43br (John Glover), 69tl (Steven Wooster), 69bl (Jerry Pavia), 69r (Sunniva Harte), 71t (Howard Rice), 72b (John Neubauer), 73tl (Eric Crichton), 73bl (Howard Rice), 73r (John Glover), 75br (John Glover), 75bl (Gary Rogers), 76b (Steven Wooster), 77bl (JS Sira), 77br (David Askham), 80 (Eric Crichton), 81l (Lamontagne), 81r (Steven Wooster), 87bl (John Glover), 96 (A. I. Lord), 97tl (Lamontagne), 97bl (Vaughan Fleming), 97r (Howard Rice), 98 (Kathy Charlton), 99tl (Vaughan Fleming), 99bl (Chris Burrows), 119bl (Jerry Pavia), 119r (Howard Rice), 119br (JS Sira).